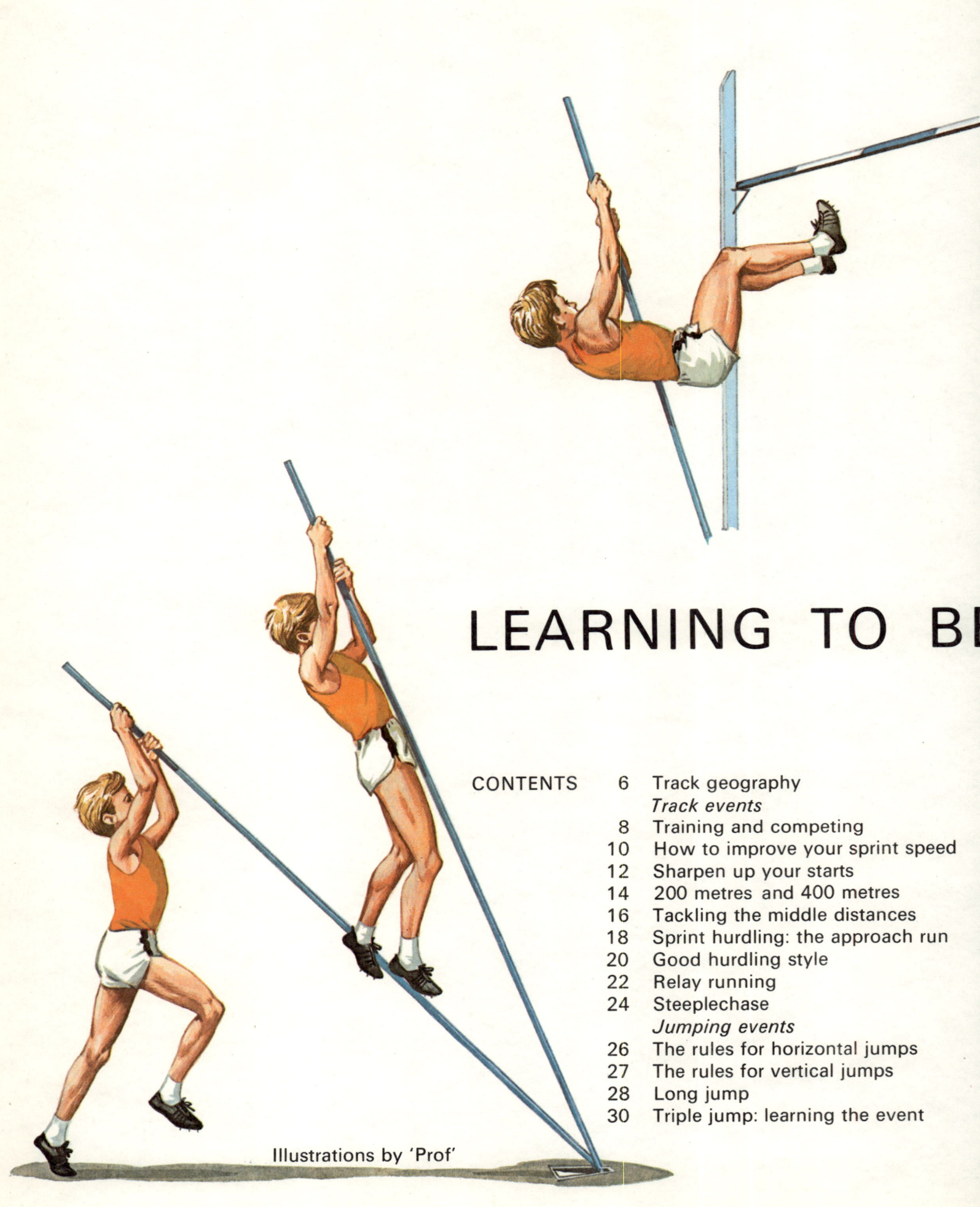

LEARNING TO BE

Illustrations by 'Prof'

A BETTER ATHLETE
all in colour

Contributors:
Track events: **John Le Masurier,**
Principal National Coach, B.A.A.B.
Jumping events: **David R. Kay,**
National Coach, B.A.A.B.
Throwing events: **Carl T. Johnson,**
National Coach, B.A.A.B.

Devised and created by Mercury Books
First published in 1975 by William Collins
Sons and Co Ltd., London and Glasgow
Copyright © Mercury Books Limited 1974
All rights reserved
Printed in Tenerife (Spain) by Litografia
A. Romero, S.A. D. L. TF 1002 - 74
ISBN 0 00 103331 X

COLLINS · GLASGOW AND LONDON

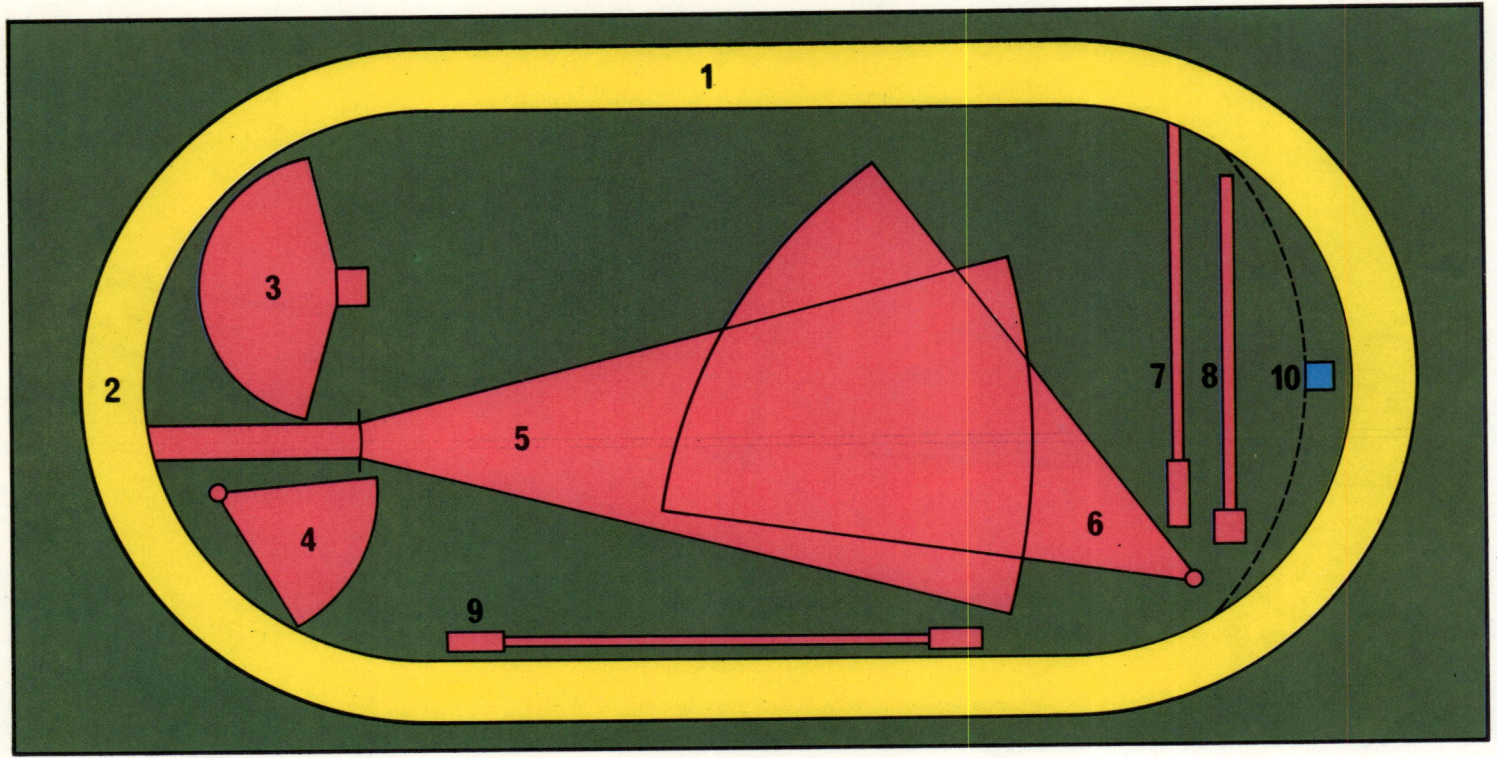

Track geography

The diagram above is a simplified plan of the standard athletics arena used, with only minor local variations, throughout the world.

The semi-elliptical running track may be of grass, cinders or a special synthetic rubber, and a full lap measures 400 metres (taken 30cm from the inside edge). Top-class tracks are now made of rubber and have the big advantage of being fast, consistent, and impervious to rain and frost. This allows athletes to train and race during the worst of winter conditions. For the jumpers this kind of surface has brought greatly improved performances and greater protection from foot injuries.

In all the track events the runners run anti-clockwise, that is, with their left side nearest the inside edge of the track.

The short sprints (100 metres and 100m/110m hurdles) are run on one of the straight sections of the track. Races up to and including 400 metres are run in lanes, each runner having to remain within his own lane for the full course of the race.

So that no runner has to run at a disadvantage the starts are staggered where necessary, so that each runner runs the exact race distance whether he has drawn an inside or an outside lane.

In the 800 metres and the 4 x 400 metres relay the first portion of the race *may* be run in lanes, with the runners being allowed to 'break' and move to the inside lane once they have passed a pre-arranged mark.

The field events take place on the grass area encircled by the running track. In some instances the pits and runways for long jump, triple jump and pole vault may be situated outside the track to allow room for team games in the central area. The jumps runways are usually sited to take account of the prevailing wind and are placed so that it blows from *behind* the athlete.

It is usual for the high jump and shot put areas to be at the 'finish' end of the arena, with the steeplechase water jump at the other end.

The surfaces of the throwing circles are made of concrete and the runways for the high jump and javelin are of the same surface material as the track itself.

Top-class arenas provide hammer/discus circles at each end of the 'back' straight, so that the throwers throw into the centre of the arena. Similarly there is usually a javelin runway at each end of the track to allow the athletes to make use of the prevailing wind.

In the course of an athletics meeting or during training sessions the arena is used simultaneously by athletes taking part in different events. It is therefore very important that everyone takes care not to get in the way of anyone else. And because the centre of the arena is a landing area for the throwing implements it is highly dangerous for runners to get into the habit of crossing it. The throwers too must take care, making sure that they do not begin their throw while anyone is in or near the possible line of flight.

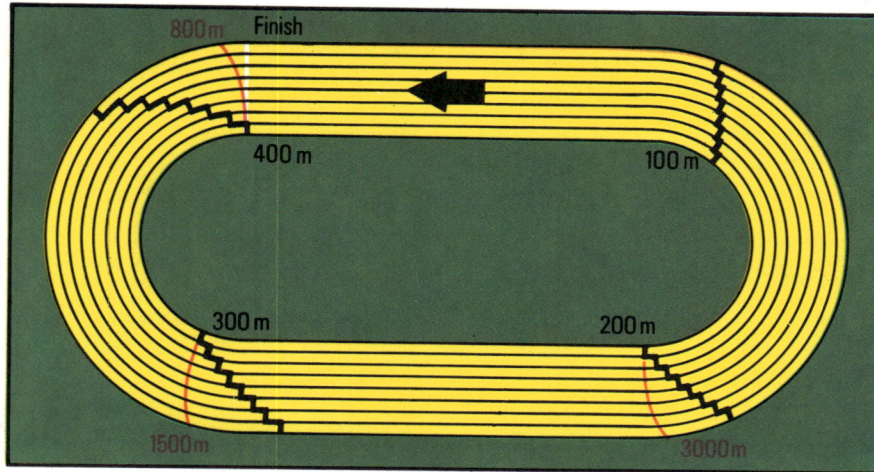

Left: a typical arena layout with a 400-metre track and a central field events area. 1. Sprint 'straight'. 2. Track. 3. High jump. 4. Shot put. 5. Javelin. 6. Discus and hammer. 7. Long jump. 8. Pole vault. 9. Triple jump. 10. Water jump.

Right: a 400-metre track showing the starting lines for track events up to 3000 metres.

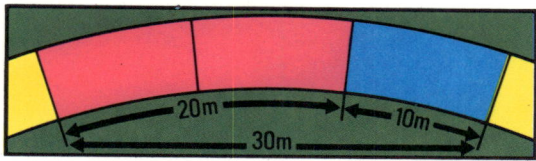

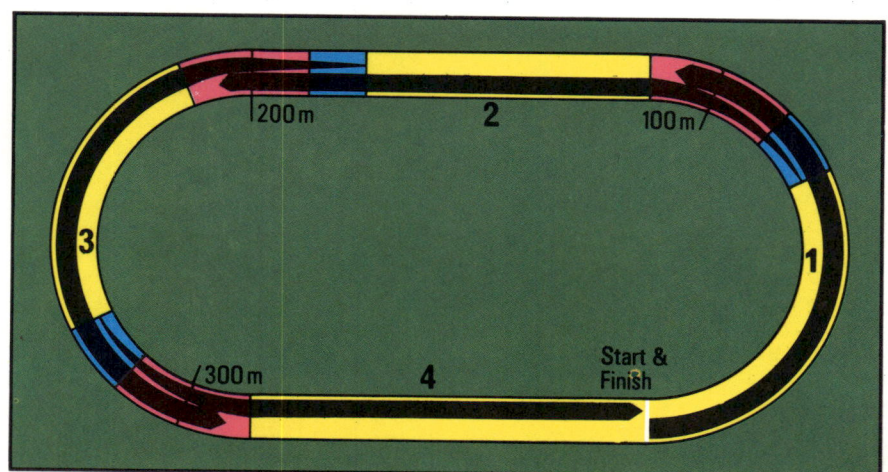

Above: take-over zone. The outgoing runner may start at any point up to 10 metres back from the take-over zone (i.e. he may start in the accelerating zone) but the baton must be passed while *both* athletes are inside the 20-metre zone.

Right: layout of a 400-metre track for the 4 × 100m relay. The red areas show the take-over zones, the blue areas the accelerating zones.

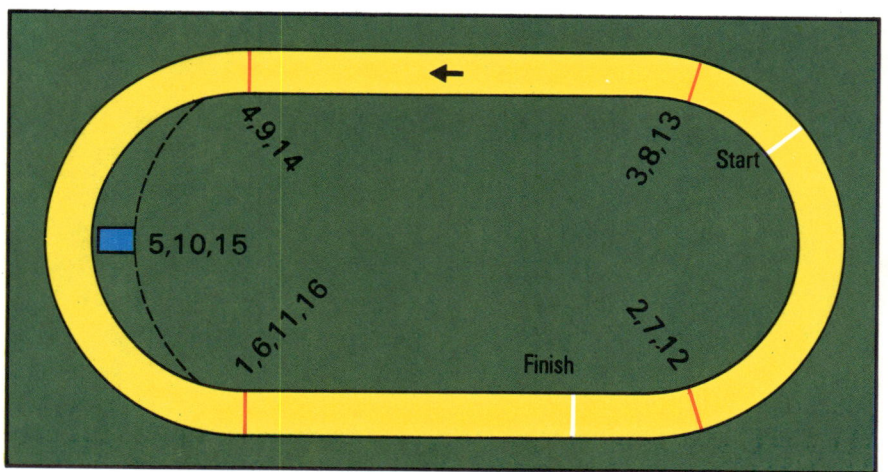

1500 metres youth steeplechase: 13 hurdles and 3 water jumps. When the water jump is set inside the track the actual lap length is reduced. For example, a 400-metre track lap is reduced to 394 metres, and the race is then run over 3 laps *plus* 318 metres.

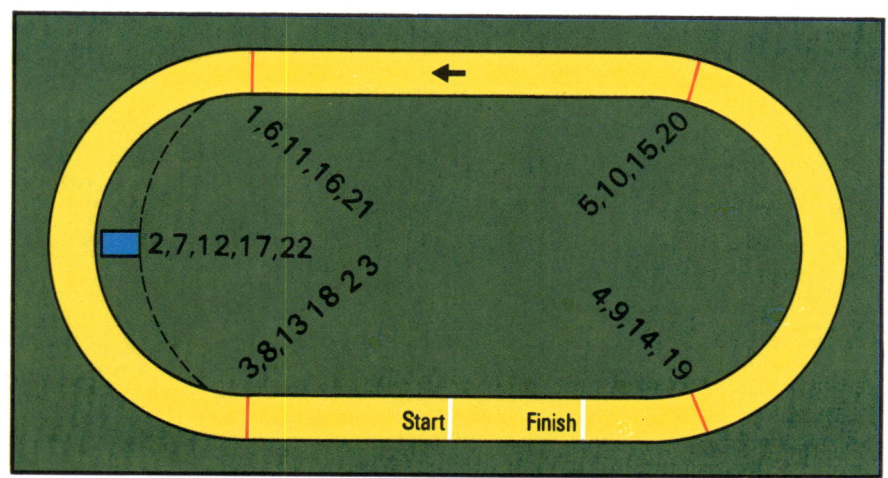

2000 metres steeplechase: 18 hurdles and 5 water jumps. On a 400-metre track with the water jump set inside the track area this race is run over 5 laps *plus* 30 metres.

Training and competing

A slim-line track suit is a neat and practical garment to keep you warm before and after a race.

Vests and shorts should be comfortable and allow complete freedom of movement. Running shoes must fit perfectly. So must socks if you wish to wear them.

Track and field athletics is the premier Olympic sport. It embraces many different events, from sprinting to hammer throwing, and from pole vaulting to marathon running. In fact it is really a multi-sport. So you should be able to find at least one event to suit you, regardless of your size or shape. Just because you aren't the fastest sprinter around doesn't mean that you can't throw a tidy javelin or put a decent shot.

Although the events are varied in character they share some common features. First, except for the relay races, they are all individual events. Secondly, provided you have a tape measure or someone to hold a stop watch for you, it is easy to measure your progress. Most of the fun, in fact, comes from measuring improvements in your own performance and from competing against other athletes of your own age. You can't all be champions, but you can all enjoy your sport and gain enormous personal satisfaction from making progress.

SKILLS AND PHYSICAL QUALITIES
To make any improvement at all you have to practise and perfect the *skills* of your chosen events. At the same time you must improve your physical qualities. Conveniently these qualities all begin with the letter S: Speed, Strength, Stamina and Suppleness. These are the key words to athletic success. You will need all of them in varying quantities.

Later on, if you begin to specialise in a particular event you will discover just how much of your training must be spent in developing these different qualities. For example, if you decide to specialise in hurdling, you must be fast, so *speed* training is essential; and to be skilful at it you must also be *supple* so that you can skim over the hurdles without wasting time floating through the air; and lastly, you must develop enough *stamina* to last the full distance of the race.

In contrast, if you decide to be a thrower, then *strength* and *speed* will be of the greatest importance.

Training shoes: for limbering up and for all preliminary work.

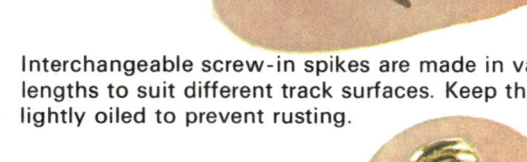

Interchangeable screw-in spikes are made in various lengths to suit different track surfaces. Keep them lightly oiled to prevent rusting.

The rules allow a maximum of six spikes in the sole and two in the heel. Heel spikes are a *must* for high jumpers and javelin throwers.

Above left: longer spikes are used on soft surfaces such as soft grass and cinder tracks.

Above right: a triangular spike, a modern development for use on synthetic tracks.

Spanners or 'keys' for changing over spikes are provided free by the shoe manufacturers.

Again, if you want to be a distance runner, the accent of your training will be on *stamina*.

LIMBERING UP

Whatever your event you should always start by doing a limbering up session for about 15 minutes. This prepares your body (and your mind) for the harder work to follow, whether it is training or competition.

Limbering up should always be carried out in warm clothing, so wear your track suit — and training shoes or gym shoes.

Start by jogging slowly for two laps of the track and then spend three or four minutes on loosening and stretching exercises. Then run for another lap of the track at a slightly faster pace and follow this by striding down the straight for 70—80 metres and repeating this two or three times.

If you are a runner, hurdler or jumper change into your running or jumping shoes at this point; if you are a thrower move to your throwing area. Complete the limber-up with more specific exercises.

Before competition you may modify this routine slightly, aiming to complete your limbering up approximately five minutes before your event is due to start.

Remember that the human body works most efficiently when it has been warmed gradually by early exercises before being put under the strain of competition.

On a point of etiquette, never run on the inside lane of the track except when you are actually racing or doing trials. This part of the track gets a great deal of use and soon becomes worn. There is also the pos-sibility of obstructing those runners who *are* doing timed runs. So do all your limbering up on the outside of the track.

COMPETITIVE ATHLETICS

When you have entered for a competition make sure that you arrive at the ground in plenty of time to check in, draw your number, change into your running gear and carry out your limbering up routine.

It takes a large number of voluntary officials to organise an athletics meeting of any kind. The most important is the *Referee*, whose job is to preside over the sports and to allocate duties to the Judges. There must be *Judges* for the track events and *Judges* for the field events.

It is also the job of the Referee to decide in the event of differences of opinion among the Judges and to deal with any points disputed under the Rules.

There must be a *Starter* and *Timekeepers*. Normally the *Starter* will wear a distinctive cap and jacket and he may be assisted by a *Marksman* whose duty is to allocate lanes and to check that all the athletes are wearing the correct numbers.

Another important official is the *Clerk of the Course,* who is responsible for seeing that the course is correctly set out and kept perfectly clear. When there are hurdle races he must check that these are correctly set out and removed after use. He also checks field event markings, and sees that the long jump boards are clean and landing areas are ready.

Stewards are responsible for issuing numbers and for making sure that the athletes are mustered ready for their competitions.

Finally, there must be *Recorders* and *Announcers*.

**leg drive
from rear foot**

stride

How to improve your sprint speed

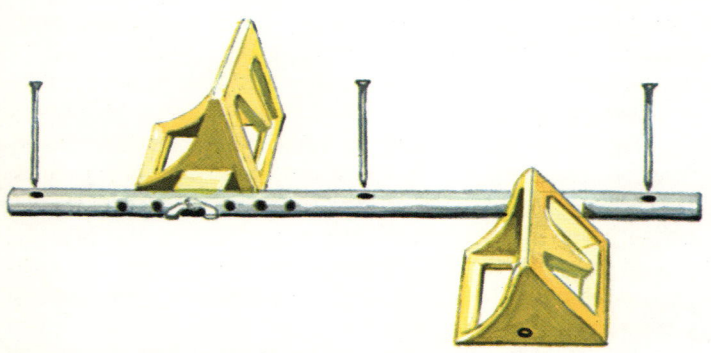

Personal starting blocks for use on cinder or grass tracks must be firmly secured by nails which you hammer into the track surface. The front support is angled at about 60° while the rear one is almost vertical and can be moved to alter the distance between your front and rear foot. On some blocks the support angles are adjustable too.

Always set your blocks absolutely securely and in a position that gives you the straightest possible run down your lane.

A good sprinter is able to run at full speed with a natural, fluent action.

There is a measure of speed in all of us; some people just have a greater measure than others. But whatever that measure we can all learn to run *faster*.

First, it is important to understand that speed is produced by the combination of your *stride length* and the rate at which you can move your legs (this is sometimes called *cadence*). Therefore, to improve your speed you have to improve either your stride length or your leg rate — or both.

STRIDE LENGTH

Let us suppose that your natural stride length measures 2 metres from toe mark to toe mark, and let us also suppose that you take, say, 50 strides to run 100 metres. If you can improve the length of each of these strides by the small amount of 5cm you will cover 2.5 metres further in the same time (50 x 5cm). This assumes that your leg rate remains the same in each case.

An improvement of 2.5 metres in a 100 metres race is enough to bring you up from last place to first.

HOW TO INCREASE STRIDE LENGTH

A good sprint stride consists of a powerful pushing action from first one leg and then the other, each straightening out behind your hips at the end of the push. This is called *driving*. In an efficient sprint stride your driving leg straightens at the knee and ankle until it is fully extended (you can see how straight it is in the illustration). At the same time the other leg swings through *fast and high* in front, giving you 'knee lift'.

bend knee

drive and knee lift

In your practices concentrate on getting this straight leg behind your hips and high knee lift in front. Practise it over short distances of about 30-40 metres, concentrating on the quality of each stride. (It helps to think of running with your thighs.)

In trying to increase your stride length, your running must remain as natural and as stylish as possible, with your legs moving forwards and backwards down a straight line. Run on the broad part of your feet and with each foot pointing straight ahead.

You will probably lose a certain amount of leg speed while you are working on improving your stride length. However, when you come into a race, your leg speed will return, although you must then expect to lose a little of your newly-found stride length.

LEG SPEED
Leg speed practices in which you try to move your legs really *fast* are also important. Speed skipping and running down a very slight gradient are two useful exercises.

LASTING THE DISTANCE
There is little point in developing an efficient stride length and smooth running style unless you can last the course.

In the example just described you were assumed to be taking 50 strides to cover 100 metres. Your aim must be to make *every one of those strides* as effective as possible so that your stride length and leg rate are as good over the last 20 metres as they are over the first 20.

As you move up from 100 metres to racing over 200 metres and, later, over 400 metres, the number of strides you will take to cover these distances will be at least doubled and quadrupled respectively. You will then have to learn how to maintain speed over the full distance by spreading your energy economically.

THE ARM ACTION
Think of your arms as the pendulum of a clock: if the pendulum is long, the 'ticks' will be *slow* (in fact they will be 'tocks') but if the pendulum is *short* the ticks will be quick. In sprinting you want a short pendulum effect because you want *speed*. So bend your arms to a right angle to make them short and fast moving.

As you run, swing your arms forward until the fingers are at shoulder level and then back until your thumb touches your hip bone. A little inwards swing is acceptable, but avoid an exaggerated cross-body action.

Don't clench your fists; keep the muscles as relaxed as possible.

Try this arm action in front of a mirror, moving your arms through the full range from shoulder to hip and back again as fast as possible. Remember that although your legs are the limbs which drive you along, your arms are also important in helping your legs to move fast and to prevent your shoulders from twisting as you run.

A good sprinter must keep his arm and leg actions in perfect time with each other.

YOUR HEAD POSITION
When you are running at top speed try to keep the muscles in your face and neck as relaxed as possible, and look forward all the time. It is a golden rule *never* to look back or sideways at any time during a sprint race.

Sharpen up your starts

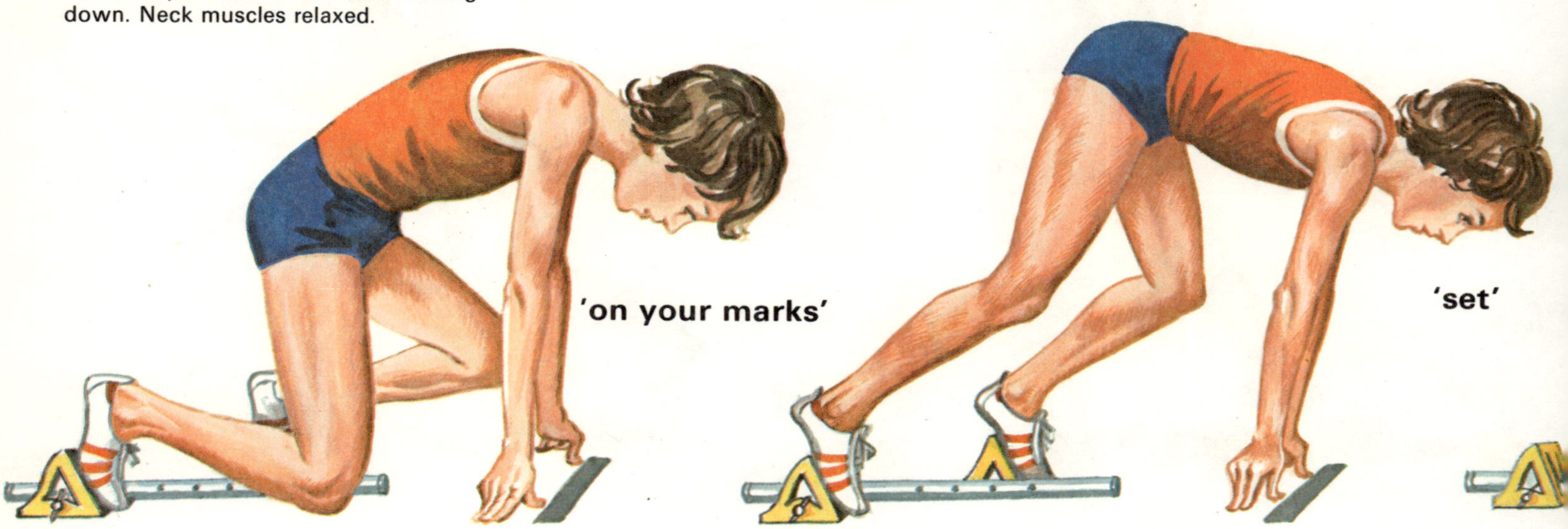

Feet firmly in the blocks. Head looking down. Neck muscles relaxed.

'on your marks'

Absolutely steady. Legs opened out with front knee at an angle of 90°.

'set'

A successful sprinter has to learn to start like a shot from a gun, and *at* a shot from a gun; the shorter the race the more important the start is.

There are two basic starts: the *standing start* and the *crouch start*. The standing start is used mainly by middle distance runners and by a *few* sprinters, while the crouch start is the common method used for sprint distances up to 400 metres. To begin with, however, it is best to learn the standing start and then, later on, you can progress quite easily to a crouch start. This change is advisable only when you own a pair of spikes, for without them your feet will slip, especially on grass.

THE STANDING START
Before a race it is usual for the competitors to assemble behind a line three metres back from the starting line to wait for the starter to give his orders. It is at this moment that you must concentrate *hard*. Try to ignore the other competitors and fix your mind on the starter and his instructions.

When he gives the command 'On your marks' walk forward and toe the starting line (but without actually touching it). Adopt the position shown in the illustration on the right, comfortably relaxed with hands resting on your thighs, and legs flexed (bent). On the starter's next command, 'Set', take your hands from your knees and move your weight forward until you can just keep your balance. This is quite a difficult position to hold and must be practised until you are confident that you can be steady. The starter will not

fire the gun until he is satisfied that *all* the competitors *are* steady. If you move before the gun is fired you may be warned the first time and disqualified the second time. In other words, you lose the race before you've started.

When the gun is fired you must react immediately. Try to get your arms working very quickly and at the same time bring your rear leg through *fast* for the first stride. If your right leg is the rear leg then your left arm must punch forward and your right arm must drive backwards. If, however, your left leg is the rear leg, then your *right* arm must punch forward and your *left* drive backwards.

Young athletes frequently make the mistake of trying to take the first stride with the *front* foot. Avoid doing this. The first step *must* be made with your rear foot.

For the first five or six strides you should be leaning forward, rising gradually until your body is upright. At the same time your strides — which should be short to begin with — will gradually lengthen as your body rises. It should take about 15–20 metres to assume an upright running position.

THE CROUCH START
For a good crouch start, measure back from the starting line the length of your foot plus the width of four fingers. Place the toes of your front foot at this point, kneel down and place the knee of your other leg opposite the toes, leaving a space between your knee and foot.

The gun has fired. Arms move swiftly. Right thigh is pulled through *fast*.

'off!'

Drive off the block. Full extension of your left knee and ankle. Your upper body is kept low.

leg drive off block and arm action

Place your hands behind the starting line with your fingers turned outwards and thumbs inwards. Look down just ahead of the line.

This is the 'on your marks' position.

If you are using starting blocks, set them about 5cm further back from the line than the position just described. For starting on the *straight,* line them up so that you run·down the *centre* of the lane; throughout the race you must keep to your own lane.

The rules require part of each foot to be in contact with the track surface when the gun fires.

On the command 'Set' raise your seat (as shown in the drawing). This has the effect of opening out your legs so that they can immediately project you forward when the gun is fired.

A common mistake is to place the front foot too close to the line so that when the gun fires your legs drive you upwards instead of *forwards*.

A good 'set' position throws quite a strain on your hands and fingers, so practise moving into this position and holding it *rock steady* while you count slowly to five.

When the gun fires you must start thrusting immediately with your legs against the blocks. As they project you forward your legs will be greatly assisted by a vigorous arm action.

Instant reflex action is the secret of fast starting. With practice the slightest sound should be all that is needed to trigger you off. The whole action of starting must become automatic and truly *explosive*, shooting you down the track.

standing start 'on your marks'

200 and 400 metres

Starting on a bend (above): angle yourself to run in a straight line before you reach the curve by placing your starting blocks slightly off-set from the centre of your lane.

The 200 metres and 400 metres are normally run in lanes, which means that at the start the competitors are in *echelon,* or in a 'staggered' start as it is generally called. The runners who draw the inside lanes start behind those in the outside lanes.

Although each athlete runs precisely the same distance, many runners prefer to draw one of the inside lanes so that they can keep an eye on their opponents during the early stages of the race and so judge their own effort more accurately.

However, as you have no control at all over the draw for lanes it is wise to develop an attitude of confidence towards all of them. Remember that important races are run – and won – every day by athletes running in outside lanes as well as the others, and that the distance you run is the same in all of them.

STARTING STRIDES
In both races the start is on the bend so you must adopt an 'on your mark' position angled towards the inner line of your lane, as shown in the illustration above. This allows your first strides to be made in a straight line, which produces better balance and more effective acceleration.

Practise starting and running into the bend in all the lanes so that you know what you have to contend with in races.

CURVE RUNNING
Practise running round the curve at different speeds, aiming to run about 15cm out from the inside line of your lane. If you run on or over the line the Referee may disqualify you.

A good practice is to jog along the back straight and gradually accelerate into the bend, building up your speed so that as you reach the crown of the turn you are travelling very close to top speed.

In both the 200 metres and 400 metres half of the race distance is contested on the bend. So unless you are a competent bend runner it will prove a handicap.

It is a skill that has to be practised. Try to maintain a flowing, relaxed stride and lean into the bend slightly. Resist the natural tendency to shorten your stride.

EXTENDED SPRINTS

Both races are extended sprints. However, if you are under 13 years old and are already running in 400-metre races, you should tackle the distance like a middle distance race and not as a sprint. This means that after the start you should settle into an easy relaxed action and save some energy for a final sprint effort over the last 50 metres.

For older and more experienced runners both races require a really fast start to build up speed, followed by a settling down period at a controlled pace.

PACE JUDGMENT

It is essential for you to learn just how fast you can run without slowing down too much at the end of the race. A knowledge of pace is particularly important in the 400 metres.

Practise running 100 metres and 150 metres in a controlled manner, trying to run fast with good style.

Set yourself pace judgment exercises so that you know the speed at which you are running. If you are aiming to run a 400 metres in 60 seconds, then you must be an expert in even-paced running. Run a series of 100 metres in 15 seconds, 150 metres in 22.5 seconds, 200 metres in 30 seconds, 300 metres in 45 seconds and so that when you are competing in a race you can 'flow' over the ground smoothly and confidently at that pace.

Control over the last part of both the 200 and 400 metres is important because your legs will be tired. Good advice here is to try to maintain your best possible style, however tired you are, and particularly to keep your arms and legs working to help one another.

Use your training practices to develop this ability to maintain style.

FINISHING

The end of all races is the finishing *line*. To be quite specific it is the edge of the line nearest to the start.

The white worsted wool (not tape) stretched at chest height over the line is there only as a help to the judges in placing the runners in the correct finishing order.

What are the judges looking for? Like a photo-finish camera, they are watching to see whose *chest* reaches the line first. Judges are not concerned with heads, necks, arms, legs or feet. At the finishing line these parts of your anatomy are unimportant; only your chest matters.

In a close finish the winner is often the sprinter who maintains a fluent style through and beyond the finishing line. No. 21 illustrates this well. Note how relaxed his shoulder, neck and face muscles are.

Tackling the middle distances

Because tactics as well as stamina help to decide the results, middle distance running is a most exciting branch of track athletics. For young athletes the most usual distances are 800 metres and 1500 metres.

STYLE
Your style should be relaxed without being sloppy. Your arm and leg movements must naturally be less forceful than when you are sprinting because in the longer races you are very much concerned with economy of effort and with saving your energy, whereas in the sprints the shortness of the event allows you to let your energy *explode*.

DEVELOPING YOUR ENGINE
A good middle distance runner is one who can run fast and maintain speed in an economical manner for the full distance of his race. It is very much like being a very efficient car that travels fast on a small amount of petrol. To become really efficient *you* have to develop a good, strong, powerful engine: your heart, your lungs and your legs!

TRAINING
To be a middle distance runner you must *enjoy* running. Find some friends who are keen to train with you. Start by building up your stamina with even-paced steady runs over short distances.

If you are young, start by running slowly for about ten minutes at a stretch. It is better to have three ten-minute runs in a week than one longer run.

This regular running will soon develop your 'engine' but if you run too far or too fast it will just make your muscles stiff. Keep to this sort of routine for three weeks, and make your running as stylish as possible with legs and arms working in perfect harmony.

From time to time vary the course you take, sometimes exploring new routes through woods or over heathland or sand dunes.

Left: the leader of this group is free from trouble but No. 2 and, to a lesser extent, No. 3 are perhaps better able to relax, knowing that if the leader decides to increase the pace they can easily go with her. Also, should they wish to speed up the pace, they can move up without obstruction. No. 1 and No. 10 (in the green vest) are 'boxed in' and could be in difficulty if they find themselves in this position in the final sprint where there must be a clear run through.

FAST AND SLOW

This start to your stamina training should gradually lead to variations of fast and slow running. This method of training over the countryside at alternately fast and slow speeds is known as 'Fartlek' (Swedish for 'speed play'). The same sort of training on the track is usually known as 'interval running', that is, fast runs interspersed with intervals of slower running.

Let us suppose that you are an 800-metre runner aiming to race to a target time of 2 minutes 40 seconds. As you can see from the chart below, each 100 metres should be covered in 20 seconds. You must practise running at this speed over different distances, e.g. 40 seconds for 200 metres, 1 minute 20 seconds for 400 metres, and so on. You must learn to judge your pace accurately.

A track training session might consist of running 200 metres in 40 seconds with a slow jog interval of 200 metres to recover, repeating this five or six times. In this way you will accustom yourself to running at the pace required for an 800 metres in 2 minutes 40 seconds.

TACTICS

Training and getting yourself fit to race is one thing; the tactics of the race is another. Tactics really means keeping your wits about you during the race.

Don't run wide round the bends. If you run in the second lane throughout an 800-metre race you will have covered an *extra* 14 metres by the time you cross the finishing line.

In most senior competitions the early stages of 800-metre races are run in lanes, with competitors 'breaking' for the inside lane after covering 300 metres. Junior races are usually started with all the competitors behind the same starting line so it is particularly important to position yourself well *as soon as the gun fires.* The start is normally close to the bend and this can cause trouble; so try to get clear of the main bunch of runners and avoid being knocked.

If you are really confident you can go straight into the lead, but it is probably best to make for a point just behind the leader and slightly out — a position known as 'on his shoulder'. From this position you can dictate the speed of the race.

Avoid being boxed in by other runners. If you do find yourself unable to extricate yourself from a boxed-in position don't panic. Keep your cool and run as close as you can to the runner immediately in front of you. You will probably find that when you reach the bend the runner on your right-hand side will move forward or drop back. This is your moment to ease out on to the shoulder of the runner in front.

EVEN-PACED RUNNING: 800 METRES					
target times in mins/secs.	2m 50s	2m 40s	2m 30s	2m 20s	2m 10s
100 metres	21·2s	20s	18·7s	17·5s	16·2s
200 metres	42·5s	40s	35·5s	35s	32·5s
400 metres	1m 25s	1m 20s	1m 15s	1m 10s	1m 5s

EVEN-PACED RUNNING: 1500 METRES					
target times in mins/secs.	6 mins	5m 40s	5m 20s	5 mins	4m 50s
100 metres	24s	22·6s	21·3s	20s	19·3s
200 metres	48s	45·2s	42·6s	40s	38·6s
400 metres	1m 36s	1m 30.4s	1m 25·2s	1m 20s	1m 17·2s
800 metres	3m 12s	3m 00·8s	2m 50·4s	2m 40s	2m 34·4s

Middle distance running style should be relaxed and flowing. Although the action is similar to your sprinting style it is very much less forceful because your aim is to save your energy and spread it over the full distance of the race.

Sprint hurdling: the approach run

drive at hurdle

It is essential to know how many strides suit you in the approach run to the first hurdle. Practise your start and approach run over and over again until you arrive at the precise take-off point every time. You can then drive fast across the hurdle. On landing you must immediately flow into a *three-stride* rhythm between hurdles, so that each clearance is as precise and as swift as the first.

Hurdle races are really sprint races in which the competitors have to clear a set number of barriers placed at regular intervals along the course, and still try to sprint as naturally as possible in between them.

To start with don't worry too much about actual heights and distances, although sooner or later you will want to have a go in competition. Instead, concentrate on perfecting the actual clearance technique, starting with five quite low obstacles (say 60cm or 70cm high) spaced evenly over a total distance of 55 metres. Later you will be expected to race over a specified course, usually with eight hurdles to be cleared in a junior course and ten in senior events.

FOOTWEAR

As you have to drive with great force both at the start and in crossing the hurdles, it is important to wear spiked shoes, especially if you are practising on grass or if the surface is at all damp. It is quite impossible to hurdle well if there is any chance of slipping.

At the beginner stage it will give you confidence if you wear shoes with spikes in the heels as well as in the soles.

USE LIGHT HURDLES

It is best to practise over *light* hurdles. Simple but practical ones can be made from three bamboo canes, two heavy plant pots, two clothes pegs and a few corks, as shown in the illustration. With this 'home-

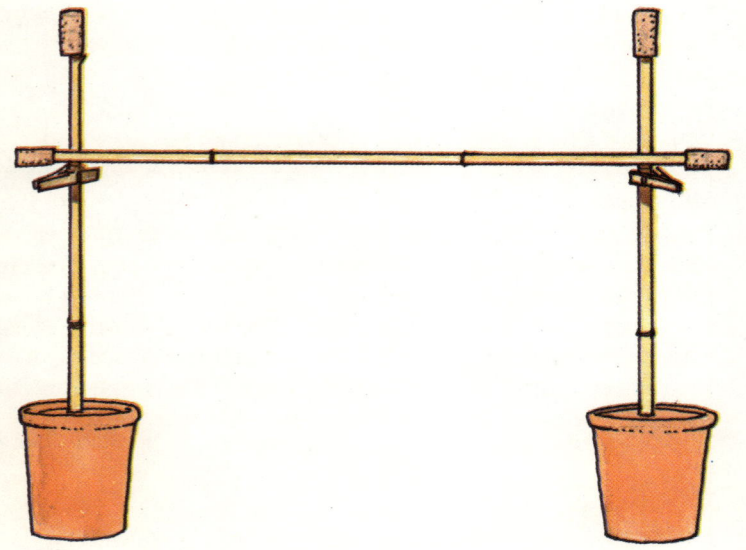

A simple but practical home-made hurdle.

lean forward for the clearance

sprint away

made' hurdle you can get some useful practice in your own garden or on the local recreation ground, starting with the 'bar' at a lowish level and gradually raising the height as you improve.

If you are able to practise over proper hurdles, make sure that you remove the weights from the supporting legs so that if you hit the hurdle it will fall easily, And always practise with the legs of the hurdles facing *towards* you. Unless you get into this habit the hurdle will knock you over instead of the other way round.

When you become more experienced and take part in hurdle races, remember that if the hurdles provided are light and unweighted you are allowed to knock down only two without being disqualified. If, however, they are of the 'international' type with counterbalancing weights on the legs, it does not matter how many you knock down *accidentally,* but if the referee considers you have knocked them down *deliberately* he will disqualify you.

Finally, it is important to remember that in crossing the hurdle you are not allowed to trail your leg or foot outside the width of the hurdle rail. If you do, you will be disqualified.

THE BASIC HURDLING ACTION
The action of crossing the hurdle is very similar to the action of stepping over a low wall. In fact, if you start by *walking* over the hurdles you will get a pretty good idea of the actual leg movements required later. Make

a special point of emphasising the sweeping action of the second ('trailing') leg.

THE APPROACH STRIDES
When you progress from walking to running over the hurdles take seven or eight sprinting strides to the first hurdle, and try to hit the same take-off point consistently. It helps to count these strides from a standing or crouch start position.

If you are tall you may need to take only seven strides, but most young hurdlers will find that eight fit best, and this means that you must have the foot of your leading leg (the one you want to swing up at the hurdle) to the *rear* in the starting position.

If you decide that your best leading leg at the hurdle is your left, then your eighth stride must be made on to the *right* foot, and the take-off point should be as much as 180cm (almost six feet) back from the hurdle.

Whichever type of start you use, try to ensure that you are *rock steady* at the 'set' position and that your movements are always consistent. This means that each time you practise the approach run your stride length must be the same. After a while you should feel so confident that you could almost run to the first hurdle with your eyes closed (but don't!).

Ideally your strides should gradually lengthen as you accelerate towards the hurdle, and at the same time your body should become more upright.

Good hurdling style

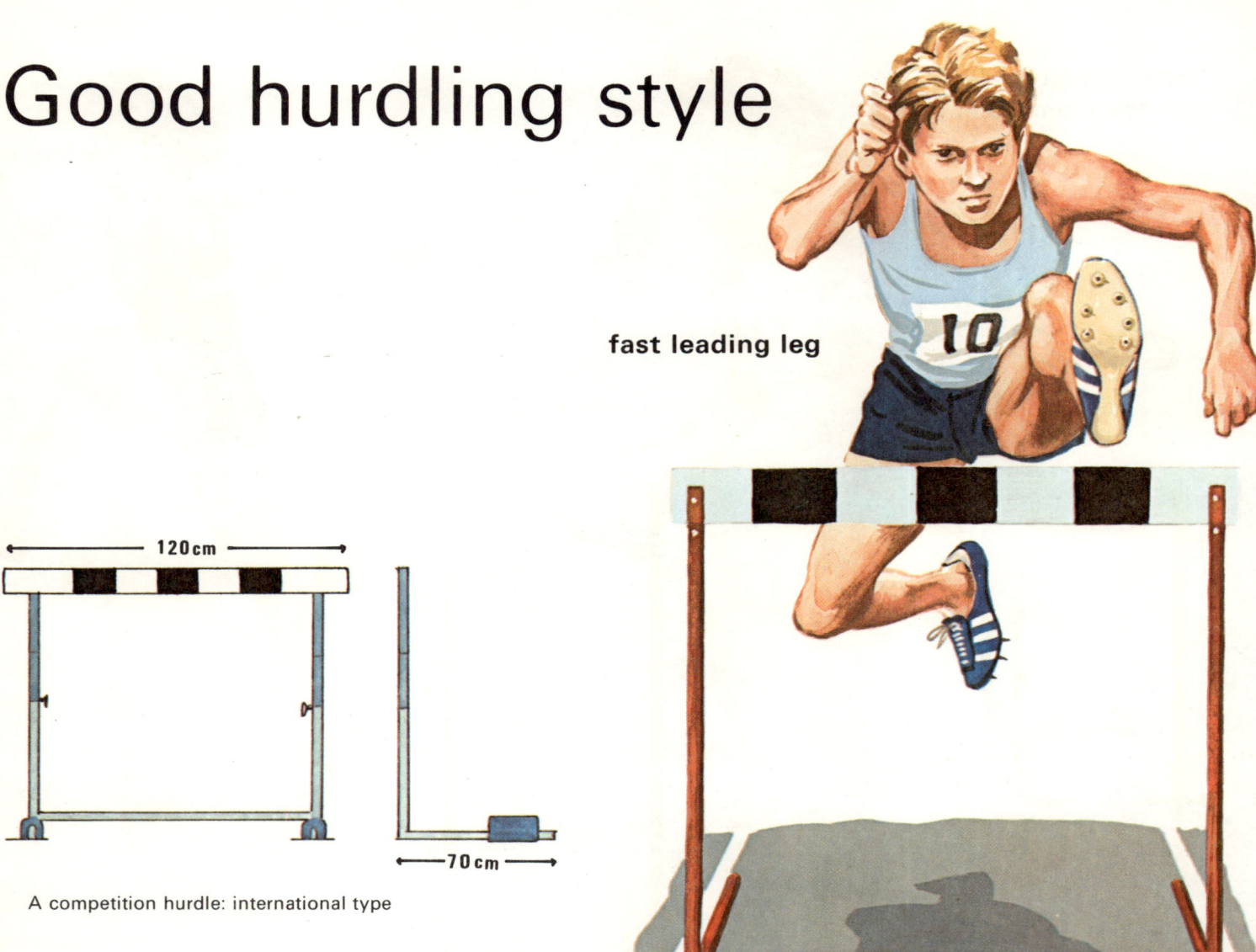

fast leading leg

120 cm

70 cm

A competition hurdle: international type

Attack your hurdle by driving *across* it. This means lifting your leading leg really fast and directly over the top of the hurdle rail. Your right arm and shoulder must drive forward too.

When you are confident about your eight-stride approach run, try taking a low hurdle in your stride.

It is wrong to refer to hurdling as *jumping.* Your aim must be to *skim* over the hurdles, *fast and low,* taking each in your stride without any hesitancy at all.

If your take-off point is well back — around 180cm from the base of the hurdle — you will find that you are able to drive yourself *across* it.

DEVELOP A FAST LEADING LEG
The most vital feature at take-off is to lift your leading leg *really fast* to clear the hurdle rail. To do this well your leg must be bent at the knee and ankle. In this way it is made into a short, fast-moving lever. Try walking around concentrating on lifting your knee high, then shooting out your foot across an imaginary hurdle.

Never think about lifting your leg 'straight' because this is a slow movement. In good hurdling the leg

will straighten out, but only because of the foot being shot out after the knee has been raised. Don't allow your leading leg to swing across your body; keep it in the line of your run.

LEAN FORWARD AT TAKE-OFF
If your drive across the hurdle is to be really efficient your chest and right shoulder must lean forward at take-off. Your right arm can be helpful here. As you take off concentrate on throwing your right hand forward and slightly towards the centre of your body. This will keep your shoulders square to the front and keep you in balance.

ROTARY ACTION OVER THE HURDLE
Your right leg must be swung in a rotary action that enables you to keep low over the hurdle. This also helps you to pick up the rhythm of your sprinting again on the other side of the hurdle. Don't duck your

skim low

Your right leg folds and sweeps sideways as you cross the hurdle. Keep your chest forward and pull your right leg through so that your thigh almost shaves the hurdle rail. Bend your right arm and sweep it back.

sweep right leg round to the front

Continue to pull your right leg through to the front so that as you touch down on your left foot you can immediately drive forward for the first stride to the next hurdle.

head — make a point of looking forward all the time.

STRIDES BETWEEN HURDLES

It is normal to take three strides between hurdles, so almost as soon as you have landed from clearing one hurdle you are preparing to take off for the next. Try to cut out anything which will slow you down. Floating gracefully through the air may look spectacular but it won't win you any prizes because it has a braking effect on your forward speed, and while you are airborne the other competitors will be powering their way to the finish. Speed is maintained by getting down to the track just as soon as possible at each clearance and keeping your arms and legs moving continuously.

Remember that hurdling is running as fast as possible over obstacles and at the same time fitting your sprinting strides as naturally as possible to the spaces between the hurdles.

HURDLES COURSES

AGE	Course distance	To first hurdle	Between hurdles	Run in	No. of hurdles	Hurdle height
Under 17						
Boys	100m	13m	8.5m	10.5m	10	92cm
Girls	80m	12m	8m	12m	8	76cm
Under 15						
Boys	80m	12m	8m	12m	8	84cm
Girls	75m	11.5m	7.5m	11m	8	76cm
Under 14						
Boys	75m	11.5m	7.5m	11m	8	76cm
Girls	70m	11m	7m	10m	8	76cm
Under 13						
Boys & Girls	70m	11m	7m	10m	8	69cm

Relay running

When within 'striking' distance the incoming runner calls 'Hand!'

The outgoing runner presents a steady right hand without slowing down and without looking back.

Relay races are usually programmed at the end of an athletics meeting and often produce a climax of excitement if the outcome of the whole competition depends on the extra points gained by the relay team. The challenge of a dropped baton or disqualification only adds to the tense anticipation.

Successful relay racing is the result of good team work. Naturally a team of four *good* sprinters has great possibilities, but a team of four *average* runners can transform themselves into a really slick squad if they are prepared to practise their baton passing.

The most usual relay event is the 4 x 100 metres.

HOLDING THE BATON AT THE START
The first runner holds the baton firmly with most of it protruding from the front of his hand. In order to adopt a comfortable 'on your marks' position it is a matter of personal preference whether you grasp it with the last *two* or the last *three* fingers. The essential thing is that the baton *must* be held safely.

THE RULES
Baton passing: the baton must be passed from the incoming runner to the outgoing runner *inside the 20-metre take-over zone* (often referred to as 'the box'). This means that at the actual moment of passing the baton *both* runners must be inside the zone, otherwise the team will be disqualified.

Ten metres back from the take-over zone there is another mark on the track, showing the beginning of the *accelerating zone*. In sprint relays the outgoing runner is allowed to start running anywhere inside this 10-metre zone in order to build up speed before entering 'the box' proper.

Senior athletes will use the whole of this extra 10 metres to pick up speed; younger runners will need rather less. The exact pick-up distance needed is something that each runner has to work out by trial and error.

THE BATON MATTERS
The whole idea in a relay is to see how fast *the baton* can cover the whole 400 metres. It is the baton that matters. As so much time can be gained (or lost) at the three change-overs the members of a relay team must practise together until their passing is really slick and confident.

If the baton is dropped it may be retrieved only by the runner who dropped it. It is best not to drop it!

METHODS OF CHANGE-OVER
First your squad must decide which method of passing to use and whether you will use left or right hands.

The most usual method is to pass the baton with an upsweeping action into the inverted V made by the receiver's waiting thumb and fingers (as shown in the small illustration). It is also usual for the first runner to carry the baton in the right hand, the second runner to receive it in the left, the third in the right, and the fourth in the left. This is known as 'the alternate pass'.

Another method, sometimes used by schools, has

the first runner with the baton in the left hand passing to the right hand of the second runner, who immediately transfers the baton to his left hand. The same pattern is followed at each change-over. So all the runners *receive* the baton in the *right* hand, and all *run* with it in the *left*.

Having decided on your method of passing you must practise as much as possible, giving particular care to placing the receiving hand in a good position *without losing speed and without looking back*. The pass should be made 'blind' – that is, *with both runners moving as near as possible to top speed and looking straight ahead.*

WHEN TO START RUNNING

The only time the outgoing runner must look round is when the baton is approaching. At this point you must adopt an efficient standing start position (*see* page 12) but looking back over your shoulder so that you can see when the incoming runner reaches a predetermined check mark. You must then look forward and at the same time sprint away at full speed.

The check mark is critical. Try using a distance of twenty foot lengths back from your starting point, making the mark very clearly visible.

Some successful school teams use the track mark that indicates the beginning of the accelerating zone as a check mark, and then measure their starting point forward into the accelerating zone.

WHEN TO PASS

Ideally the incoming runner should pass the baton to the next 'leg' in the second half of the box, and on coming within passing distance must shout 'Hand!'. On this command you should immediately swing your arm back so that your hand presents a steady, easily hit target. On no account look round or start feeling about for the baton. Your job as the outgoing runner is to keep the receiving hand still. You must have confidence that your partner will pass successfully.

Once the baton has been passed the incoming runner must stay in your team's lane until all the other teams have passed through their zones.

Smooth baton passing comes only with frequent practice. Don't be satisfied until you reach perfection.

The end of the upsweep action. The incoming hand keeps a positive hold on the baton until the outgoing runner's hand has closed firmly round it.

The baton passes smoothly while both runners are still inside 'the box'.

Steeplechase

settle

land on ba[r]

push out

There are two main steeplechase events: one over a 2000-metre course for boys of 17–20, and one over a 1500-metre course for 15–17 year olds. There are no steeplechases for girls.

COURSES
The general layout of two typical steeplechase courses is shown on page 7. The water jump may be positioned either *inside* or just *outside* the main circuit of the 400-metre track. As this shortens or lengthens the distance of the laps it is not possible to have a rule specifying the exact length of the laps. It is, however, more usual for the water jump to be just *inside* the main track, thus reducing the 400-metre lap by about 6 metres to a total 394 metres.

THE OBSTACLES
There are four steeplechase hurdles and one water jump per lap of the course. Unlike the hurdles used in hurdle races, which can be toppled fairly easily (and fairly painlessly), steeplechase hurdles are really solid, 3.66m wide and 91.4cm high.

The water jump, which has to be crossed five times in a 2000-metre race and three times in a 1500-metre race, has a solid fixed barrier in front of it with the same dimensions as the hurdles.

THE STEEPLECHASER'S RUNNING ABILITY
To be a good steeplechaser you should be an agile and resilient runner, performing well in cross-country races and with good middle distance times to your credit.

You must not be the sort of runner who is easily upset by having the rhythm of your running broken by clearing five obstacles in the course of each lap. The more easily you can maintain a steady pace with

relaxation and an even rhythm the better your performance will be.

TECHNIQUE IN STEEPLECHASE
You should use a normal hurdles clearance as described on pages 18–21, but at the water jump you should put one foot on the bar and *stride out* into the shallow end of the jump causing as little change in your rhythm as possible.

LEARNING THE EVENT
You can learn to clear the water jump by practising with a steeplechase hurdle on the track. Run up to the hurdle, put one foot on the bar and thrust off on to the track with as little hesitation as possible. Progress from this by setting the hurdle alongside the long jump area and repeating the exercise. Make sure that you have a stretch of sand at least 3.66 metres long to simulate the water jump.

This practice will help considerably and give you confidence for tackling the real thing.

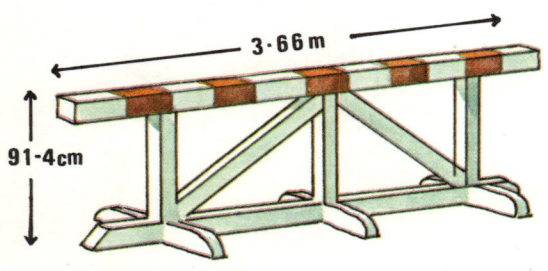

Steeplechase hurdle

3.66 m

91.4 cm

take-off

approach

push and reach

land

clearing the water jump

SPEEDING UP AND ATTACKING THE OBSTACLES

To maintain the essential running rhythm you must speed up as you approach the obstacles. 'Attack' each obstacle from about six paces out and don't chop your strides. In approaching the water jump, it helps in practice sessions to have a check mark about eight running strides out; this should be so placed as to bring you on to a take-off point about a metre and a half from the base of the barrier.

It is important to approach all obstacles with confidence. When you are sure that you can arrive consistently at your take-off point on the correct foot you will find it fairly easy to leap up and place your foot on the bar. You must then crouch over this leg and thrust strongly away from the bar as you reach out for the shallow end of the sloping water jump with the other leg. You should land on one foot. In a successful clearance, provided you have thrust off really hard against the bar with the other leg, you will flow through the water with only *one* wet foot.

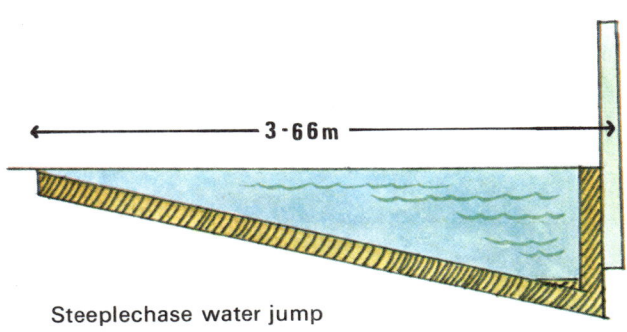

← 3·66 m →

Steeplechase water jump

The rules for horizontal jumps

There are four jumping events, two of them horizontal jumps (long jump and triple jump) and two vertical jumps (high jump and pole vault). It could be argued that the pole vault is not strictly a *jump* because an aid (the pole) is used to assist the athlete, but for practical purposes it is classified as a jump.

The two horizontal jumps are both done for distance, frequently from the same runway and into the same pit, and both attract the same type of athlete.

THE RULES: LONG JUMP AND TRIPLE JUMP
In both events take-off is from a wooden board painted white, 1.22cm long, 20cm wide and 10cm deep.

Order of jumping: this is decided by drawing lots.

Number of jumps: each competitor is allowed three attempts and is credited with the best of his three.

No jumps: it is a 'no jump' if the jumper's hands or any other part of his body touch the ground outside the pit *nearer* to the board than the mark in the sand.

It is also a 'no jump' if any part of the jumper's feet touch the ground in front of the take-off board, that is, if any part of the feet overshoots the edge of the board nearest the pit.

The tie rule: in the event of a tie the premier place is given to the competitor who has made the longest jump other than the jump which created the tie. In other words, the competitor whose second best jump is longest.

Measuring the jump: both horizontal jumps are measured in the same way: from the part of the mark nearest the take-off board to the front edge of the board. The mark may be made by any part of the jumper's body — hands, feet, even seat! The measurement is taken by placing the zero end of the tape against the mark and 'reading off' the distance jumped at the front edge of the board (i.e. the edge nearest the pit).

For accurate measurement the sand should be dampened before the pit is used, raked after every three or four jumps, and dug thoroughly periodically. It can be dangerous for jumpers to land in the feet marks of previous jumpers, or even in their own marks, because there is a risk of touching the hard bottom of the pit. In competition the pit is raked after every jump.

At the beginning of a training session it is a good idea to check in case any object lies buried in the pit. A fire extinguisher was found in one pit! As some athletic grounds allow the jumping pit to be used for shot put too (a practice which should be discouraged), inspect carefully for a buried shot that could be 'found' by the feet of a jumper.

It is also essential for the board to be flush with the runway as injuries can occur if it protrudes above ground level, especially if the board is less than the required 20cm wide. The sand in the pit should be level with the take-off board.

Alternative in-the-air techniques for long jump.

sail

hang

The rules for vertical jumps

High jump and pole vault are vertical events in which the athlete is trying to gain as much height as possible, the winner being the one who jumps highest.

THE RULES: HIGH JUMP AND POLE VAULT
Many of the same rules apply to both high jump and pole vault. The main ones are given below, and except where stated they apply to both events.

The take-off: the high jumper may take off where he chooses and he may take as long a run-up as he pleases. The pole vaulter must take off with the pole 'planted' in a wooden or metal box set in the ground in front of the vault.

Order of jumping: this is drawn by lots.

Jumping height: the judges decide the height at which jumping starts and the amount by which the bar is raised after each round.

Number of jumps: each competitor may make three attempts to clear each height until he is eliminated from further jumping by his own failures.

Failures: if a competitor has three consecutive failures then he is eliminated from the contest, regardless of the heights at which the failures occurred.

High jumps no jumps: it is a failure if in your attempt to clear the bar you:
1. dislodge the bar so that it falls from its pegs.
2. touch the ground or landing area beyond an imaginary line drawn between the uprights without

first clearing the bar, or 3. make a *two-footed* take off.

Pole vault no jumps: it is a no jump if you: 1. dislodge the bar with your body or the pole so that it falls from its pegs. 2. touch the ground beyond the vertical plane of the uprights with any part of your body or the pole before clearing the bar. 3. leave the ground to make a vault but fail to clear the bar. 4. move your lower hand above your upper hand or move the upper hand further up the pole at the moment of making the vault or after leaving the ground.

If your pole breaks as you jump it is not counted as a no jump or as a failure.

The tie rule: if two competitors tie then the premier place is given to the one who has made the lowest number of jumps at the height at which the tie occurs.

Measuring the jumps: the height is measured perpendicularly from the ground to the upper side of the lowest point of the bar.

The pole: the pole may be made of any material but the surface must be smooth. It may be any length and any diameter but its binding may not be more than two layers of adhesive tape of uniform thickness.

Posts and uprights: in high jump the posts and uprights may not be moved unless the judges consider the ground surface is unsuitable. In pole vault the vaulter may have the uprights moved by a maximum of 60cm in either direction from the prolongation of the inside edge of the top of the box.

hitch kick

Long jump

hitting the board

drive up and forward

The long jumper must be a fast runner and he must also be able to spring. In fact, long jump has been described as 'the sprint with the high jump on the end'.

THE BASIC ACTION
The basic action of the long jumper is to *run up* for a fast take-off from the board, *leap up in the air*, and *drive out* for distance. This is an aim that, even as a novice, you share with the most experienced international jumper. Your aim is the same: it is the result that differs!

As a novice avoid complicating your first efforts with matters of technique; *just try to jump as far as you possibly can.*

In the early stages of long jumping there is nothing wrong with ignoring the take-off board altogether and measuring the jump from your take-off (wherever it occurs) to your landing. This means that you will need to work with a partner who can watch for your take-off point. As you begin to get a taste for the event and become better at it, you can begin using the take-off board.

THE APPROACH RUN
How many strides should you have in your run? There is no fixed number, but a younger, shorter and slower athlete will take a shorter approach run than an older, taller and faster team-mate. Eleven or thirteen strides is approximately right for a young jumper, while an older one may well use fifteen.

A run-up that is too long can cause you to be too fast on the runway too soon, and this in its turn can produce a ragged run-up because you are straining to hold top speed. You do not reach top speed at take-off, although you come very near to it.

Too long a run makes you too fast too soon, but too *short* a run gives you too little speed off the board.

Having decided on the number of strides you will try, stand on the take-off board with your back to the pit and *at full speed* run the selected number of strides *away* from it.

A partner can mark the point at which your foot lands on the eleventh or thirteenth stride. This will give you an *approximate* starting mark – approximate because it is very rare for anyone to make exactly the same run *away* from the board as *towards* it.

Now stand on the mark with both feet together and, with your take-off foot leading, begin your run up to the board. It is then possible to count: *one, three, five, seven, nine, eleven, thirteen,* and from the final stride leap into the air.

HITTING THE BOARD
With practice you will be able to hit the board or come very near to it at every jump. But even if you fail to meet the board correctly, don't change your starting mark right away. Instead, wait until you have a sequence of misses and then adjust your mark accordingly.

The object of the run-up is to make sure that you arrive at the board *at speed*. Being slow or slowing

in the air

leg shoot

down at the board ruins any performance. You should not look down during the last few strides, and while ideally your foot should land *on* the board, make no attempt to lengthen your last stride simply to make it do so. Such an action has a braking effect and prevents you from getting off the ground.

The main thing is to make sure that your last stride on to the board is not too long and is made with your take-off foot planted flat and with a slightly bent knee.

THE DRIVE FROM THE BOARD
This is probably the most important part of the jump. Your drive should be *up* and *out*. Extend your take-off leg and bring the thigh of the other leg up vigorously until it is parallel with the ground.

ACTION IN THE AIR
Once you have launched yourself with a powerful drive off the board there are three generally recognised ways of sustaining your forward movement in the air: the *sail*, the *hang*, and the *hitch kick* (shown on page 26 and page 27).

The *sail* is the natural technique used by a novice, in which the athlete *jumps* through the air, usually with both feet outstretched ahead of him. It is a style that has weaknesses though, mainly because the jumper's heels drop before landing and so lose valuable distance.

The *hitch kick* is the technique most generally used by top-class performers but it can be difficult to learn.

The illustrations above demonstrate the *hang*, in which you must work first for a long thin shape in the air by pulling your free leg down and back, straight, to join your take-off leg. Then, keeping your chest pushed upwards, your hips pressed forward and eyes looking straight ahead, bend both knees so that your feet are behind your body. At the same time let your arms swing back and up. Try to achieve a bow shape in the air.

LEG SHOOT AND LANDING
Bring your legs forward and shoot your heels out as far in front as you can, keeping both feet level and circling your arms up and over from behind. Bend your knees as your feet hit the sand and let your arms swing through past your hips. This will help to bring your body weight forward over your feet and prevent you from sitting back in the pit. If there is enough speed in your jump you will pivot forward over your heels as you land.

Use a short approach run in your practices and perhaps a beat board to help to drive you up and out; but bear in mind that, finally, the event has to be performed without the board and after a *full* run.

GENERAL COACHING POINTS
In long jump the most important skill lies in running up fast and lifting up and out. The jump is made or marred by the quality of your approach and take-off. Your action in the air adds only a little to a result that is decided mainly by your action off the board.

Triple jump: learning the event

Practise flat-footed hopping. This absorbs the force of your landing and gives you lift off the board.

Hopping up and down steps is a good strengthening exercise to give you those 'legs of teak' needed by a triple jumper.

Many people think that the triple jump is a slightly comical event. There is nothing comical however about the men who compete in this tough 3-phase event. They have to be strong, fast and skilful – real athletes. There is no triple jump for women or girls, although many use the practices of the triple jumper in training for long jump.

The triple jump is a very popular event with young athletes, possibly because the distances that can be achieved are greater than in long jump and therefore more satisfying.

THE RULES

The rules for triple jump are quite simple: they are the same as for long jump with two additional 'no jump' situations: there must be a correct sequence in the action, that is, there must be a *hop*, followed by a *step*, followed by a *jump*. If a triple jumper performs the actions in the wrong order then a 'no jump' is recorded. There is also a 'sleeping leg' rule: if the leg that is not being used (the 'sleeping' leg) touches the

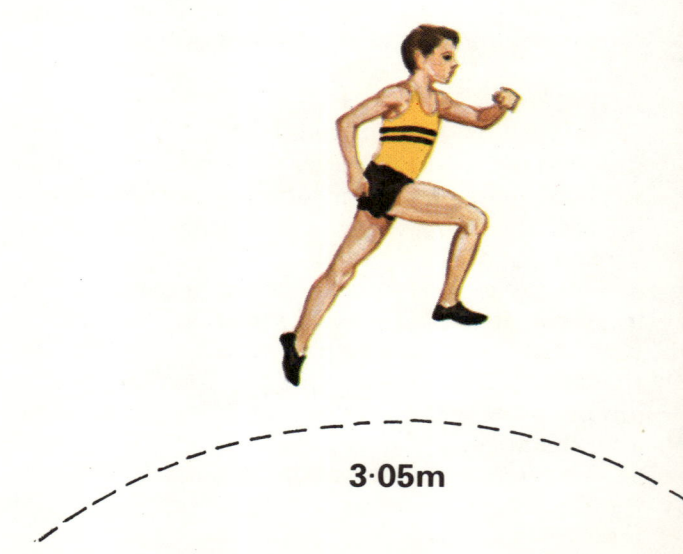

3·05m

ground during the course of the three phases, then a 'no jump' is called.

SAFETY IN TRIPLE JUMPING
The triple event must never be practised in bare feet because the jarring action can damage your heels. Jumping shoes with specially padded heels give the best protection. For extra protection top-line jumpers often slip nylon heel cups into their shoes.

An uneven surface can also cause injury, so grass which has been pitted by the feet of other jumpers should be avoided, especially if it has hardened.

LEARNING THE BASIC ACTION
Triple jumping is a flat-footed event, except of course for the run-up, which you make with a sprint action. But in the learning stages forget about the run-up and practise from a *standing start*. First, stand on one leg (it doesn't matter which) and *hop* so as to land on the *same* leg, then *step* on to the *other* leg, and then *jump* on to *both*. Repeat this again and again, saying to yourself: SAME – OTHER – BOTH.

If you then repeat the sequence time after time, concentrating hard on planting your feet *very flat*, you will have the basis on which to build a good triple jump.

RHYTHM IS IMPORTANT
Correct rhythm is essential for a triple jumper, not because the rhythm itself is important but because it ensures that the three phases (the hop, the step, *and* the jump) are equally balanced. No single phase is more important that either of the others. The hop is always *longer* than the step but not more important.

Once you have learned the technique of planting your feet flat and getting the correct *same-other-both* sequence, the rhythm should be *dah-dah-dah* – three even beats. The best way to learn it is by setting yourself targets. Place a shoe, a peg or some other mark on the ground to give you a starting mark. Then set further marks at 1 metre and 2.5 metres. Stand at the starting mark *on one leg* and *hop* to the 1-metre mark, then *step* on to the other leg at the 2.5 metre mark, and finally *jump* as far as you possibly can beyond the 2.5 metre mark *on to both feet*.

You may find these distances disappointingly easy, but don't be tempted to go beyond the marks. Keep repeating the phrase SAME – OTHER – BOTH as you go through the action. When you are landing on flat feet each time, you are ready to increase the distances between the marks. The table below will act as a rough guide:

Hop to	Step to
1 metre	2.50 metres
1.20 metres	2.70 metres
1.40 metres	3.00 metres
1.50 metres	3.20 metres
1.70 metres	3.50 metres
2.00 metres	4.00 metres

TRY A ONE-STRIDE APPROACH
As soon as you find it difficult to hop to the first mark, begin with a step on to the starting line, thus substituting a *one-stride approach* for your standing start. This will help you to generate more speed and to reach longer distances.

If you leave your original marks in position your progress will be very clear when you find that your hop is being made on to the mark you originally set down for the *step*.

A few words of warning though. Don't exceed the distances given in the table even if you find it easy to do so. And keep the hop under control. Anyone can produce a long, high hop but it is all too easy to collapse after it, and this makes the step short — something that isn't wanted. The *dah-dah-dah* then become the unwanted *dah-dit-dah*.

A useful reminder of what is wanted is:
The hop is low – the jump higher – the step highest.

LENGTHENING YOUR APPROACH RUN
As the distances between your starting point and the marks increase you will be tempted to take a run at the starting line. This is a natural advance at this stage. But resist the temptation to take too long a run-up: 3, 5 or 7 strides are good numbers to work off while you are still learning the skills of the event. Bear in mind that the more speed you generate on your run-up, the greater the strength you need to take up the force at the end of the hop.

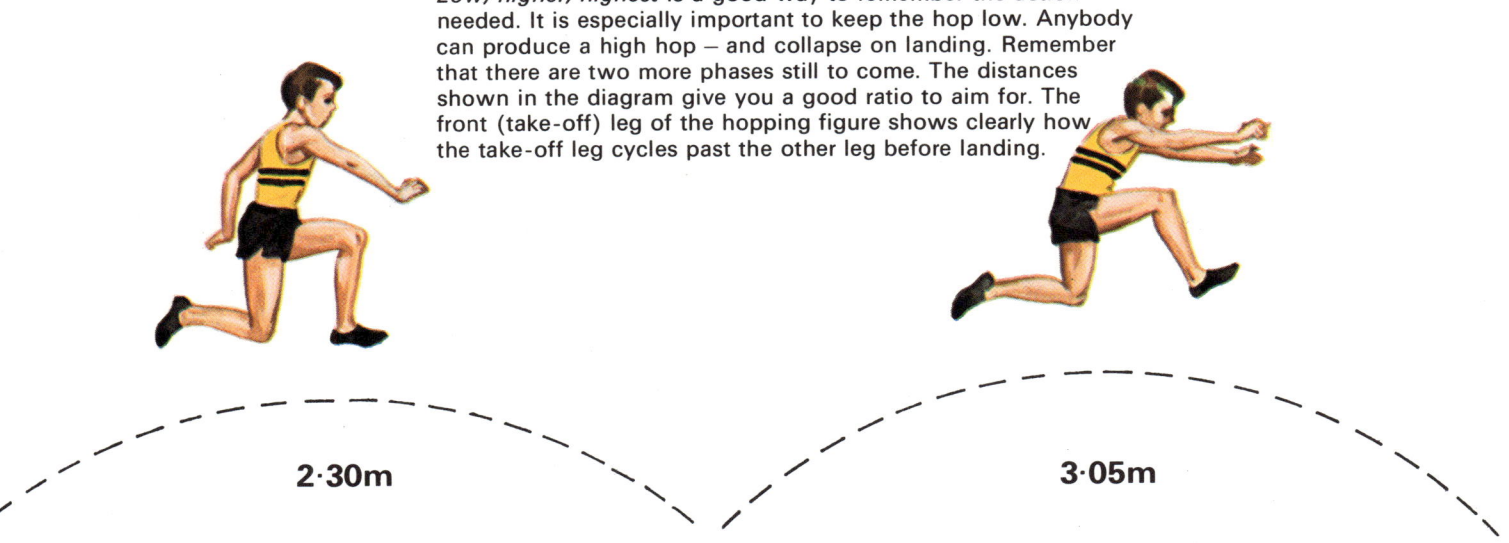

Low, higher, highest is a good way to remember the action needed. It is especially important to keep the hop low. Anybody can produce a high hop — and collapse on landing. Remember that there are two more phases still to come. The distances shown in the diagram give you a good ratio to aim for. The front (take-off) leg of the hopping figure shows clearly how the take-off leg cycles past the other leg before landing.

2·30m   3·05m

land from step

jump

step

Triple jump

THE HOP
Many novices start hopping on a stiff leg. This is something a triple jumper must never do. Your take-off leg *bends* and is therefore *active* on landing, absorbing the weight of your body and ready to thrust off into the step phase. In fact, between take-off and landing your hopping leg bends so sharply that your thigh should be parallel to the ground.

A prospective triple jumper must, then, do plenty of hopping practice with an *active* hopping leg, bending the knee on each hop. At this stage hopping short distances is too easy, so aim to make each hop *up* and *out* for distance. Try ten hops with knee bending. As the hops progress you will get a feeling of 'cycling' with the hopping leg. Avoid the danger of making the hops on to your *toes*. Train yourself to perform a flat-footed hop *every time*.

Your non-hopping foot contributes nothing to the action at this stage and can be ignored. For the novice (and for many top-line jumpers too) the arms balance the legs in all three phases. The body should remain upright and balanced and must not pike (bend).

THE STEP
A long, high hop and little else to follow except a step that helps you to recover is *poor* technique. Olympic performers manage to add as much as 5.2 metres to their distance with their step. Your performance will also benefit (though not as much!) if you develop a good step phase.

A good step comes from combining *leg strength* and *skill*. After landing from the hop you should actively think 'knee up', which means getting the thigh of your non-hopping leg through and parallel to the ground. A good technique gives a good 'split' between the thighs, and it is best if the heel of your leading leg does not poke ahead of your knee.

You gain distance in the step by letting the momentum of the hop carry you forward, holding your stepping leg off the ground as long as possible. But in no circumstances should you stretch your stepping leg out to achieve greater distance. Poking it forward as it comes to land has a braking effect, and at this stage it is important to keep your forward speed.

When you are an experienced jumper (and not until) you will learn to pull the heel of your stepping leg towards the rear of your thigh. This 'knee squeezing' effect must not take place until your thigh is parallel with the ground, otherwise it makes your step less efficient. Don't try to use the knee squeeze until you have learned the rest of the step technique.

THE JUMP
On landing from the step, you have to lift yourself *up* and *out* to complete the jump. Some athletes are content to 'sail' into the pit, others prefer to 'hang'.

drive into step

land on bent leg

hop

he three phases

There is no set length for the approach run but it is usually an odd number of strides. A younger, shorter, slower jumper generally takes a shorter run than an older, taller and faster team-mate. Make the first step of your run on to your take-off foot and then count every other stride: *one, three, five, seven* and so on until you reach the board.

LANDING

As your overall technique improves you can lengthen your run-up, but restrict it to 11, 13 or 15 strides — no more. It is just not possible to manage three good phases if your leg strength cannot take the speed from a long run-up. So keep the run short, the rhythm smooth, and an even balance in all three phases.

USEFUL TRAINING

A triple jumper's training has to be geared to produce equal strength in both legs. All hopping and bounding exercises, and combinations of hopping, stepping and jumping are useful.

Try using the 'jumps pentathlon' table *(right)* to help you to train. You will soon be measuring improvements in the distances you achieve and the points you score.

JUMPS 'PENTATHLON' (DISTANCES IN METRES)

Points	SLJ	STJ	2HSJ	2H2SLJ	2H2S2J
60	2·40	8·00	9·30	11·50	14·00
50	2·30	7·50	8·80	11·00	13·00
45	2·10	7·00	8·50	10·50	12·20
40	2·00	6·50	7·80	9·90	11·20
35	1·80	6·00	7·30	9·20	10·80
30	1·70	5·50	6·80	8·70	10·00
25	1·50	5·00	6·30	8·00	9·45
20	1·40	4·50	5·80	7·50	8·80
15	1·25	4·00	5·30	7·00	8·30
10	1·00	3·50	4·80	6·50	7·80

SLJ: *standing long jump*, STJ: *standing triple jump*, H: *hop*, S: *step*.

High jump: clearance styles

Scissors

The take-off for scissors is made from your *outside* foot, planted *flat*. Although it is an excellent way to learn the essentials of high jumping it is less efficient than other techniques because you have to raise yourself higher in the air to clear the bar.

In scissors the jumper approaches the bar from an acute angle (about 20° to 30°), drives off the ground with his take-off (outside) foot to get height, and swings his free leg over the bar. The free leg is, then, the first leg into the sand.

To get height you have, obviously, to drive upwards with your take-off leg. To do this you must land *flat-footed* on the last stride of your run-up, with your take-off leg in a *bent* position. Then straighten the leg vigorously. Too many novice jumpers just run up and then continue to run off the ground, still on their toes and quite unable to drive upwards.

FREE LEG SWING
You can get some idea of what free leg swing does without jumping at all. Stand quite still and throw a straight leg in the air. You will feel as though you are being lifted off the ground, and will need no further demonstration of how free leg swing helps to give you lift off! But do it cautiously as it is fairly easy to throw yourself on to your back!

THE 3-STRIDE APPROACH
In the learning stage use a three-stride approach. Your take-off position should be roughly an arm's length from the bar, but not in the centre of the bar. Aim instead for a take-off towards the upright on the approach side. So, if you are approaching from the left, try to take off near the left-hand upright, and if you are making an approach from the right, try to take off near the right-hand upright.

You can get an *approximate* take-off position by taking three *running* strides *away* from the bar at a fairly narrow angle. But it will be no more than an approximate mark, which you will learn to adjust.

The only way to check whether you have got your starting position correctly fixed is to get someone else to watch to see whether the high point of your jump occurs (as it should) *directly over the bar*, or just in front of it or just beyond it. You can then make what adjustments are needed in repositioning your starting mark.

In the scissors, take-off is on your *outside* foot (the foot furthest from the bar). In the early stages get used to saying: *left, right, left* or *right, left, right* for the three strides, depending on which take-off foot you use.

INCREASE TO A FIVE-STRIDE APPROACH
You should soon be ready to move your starting mark out to a five-stride approach (again measuring back from the bar as you did to fix your three-stride approach mark). But don't be in too big a hurry to move out to seven strides, and don't attempt anything more than that. The extra speed you would generate in your run-up would cause problems in your take-off as your bent leg would probably buckle under you and **prevent** a good lift.

The **first two** strides should be on your toes, the last three *on flat feet*.

THE WEAKNESS OF SCISSOR JUMPING
Because you have to adopt a more or less upright sitting position as you cross the bar, you have to lift your hips much higher than in any other technique in order to clear your legs. All the same, scissors is a good style for learning the fundamentals and language of high jumping.

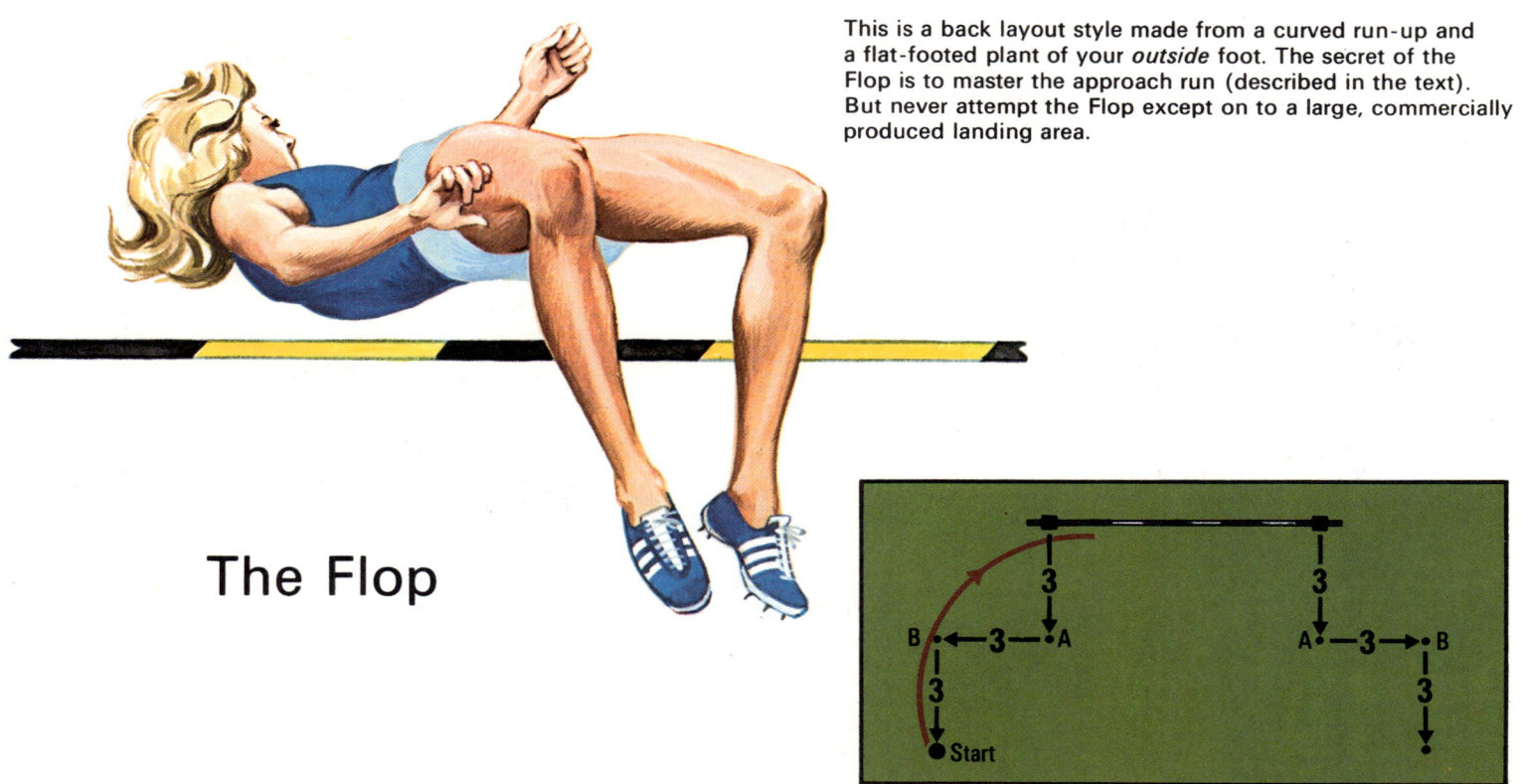

This is a back layout style made from a curved run-up and a flat-footed plant of your *outside* foot. The secret of the Flop is to master the approach run (described in the text). But never attempt the Flop except on to a large, commercially produced landing area.

The Flop

The curved approach run for the Flop.

The Flop is an exciting back layout technique now very much in fashion and every young high jumper is keen to have a go at it especially as it offers rapid improvement in the heights jumped.

But it must be stressed again that many landing areas are totally unsuitable for the Flop. Flopping must *never* take place into sand, and landing beds must be big enough to prevent missing, and dense enough to prevent bottoming. The Flop landing is made on shoulder blades, shoulders and neck, and it needs very little imagination to see that serious injury can occur if bottoming or missing the bed are even remotely possible.

THE FLOP ACTION
The Flop is not, as at first it seems, a *backward* jump, even though you clear the bar head and back first. The take-off is made, as in scissors, off the *outside* foot. And, as in all high jumping styles, it is a *flat-footed* take-off at the end of a run designed to get you to the bar at speed. It must be made at or close to the upright.

Because the Flopper travels *along* the bar, it is very easy to 'run out of bed'. So, if you have not started your take-off by the time you reach the centre of the bar, you must 'kill' the jump and start again.

LEARNING THE APPROACH
Start with a five-stride approach, in a curving run as shown in the diagram on this page.

Stand with your back against the upright and walk three strides away from it, then mark point *A*, as shown. Next turn at right angles and take three more strides to point *B* and mark that. Finally, turn at right angles again and walk three strides to get your starting mark.

The mark *B* is an important one, as your curved run will sweep round just outside it.

Although the marks *appear* to put you *six* strides away from the bar, they are *walking* strides and are equal to *five* running strides.

You must increase your speed after you have passed mark *B* and as you begin the curved run in. Don't let the run get 'flat' or you will arrive at the upright in the wrong position for Flopping. So avoid making a straight-line run. The correct run-up is more like an inverted letter J.

When you can manage the five-stride approach fairly well, you can move out to a seven- or nine-stride approach.

PUTTING THE TURN IN THE FLOP
The Flopper does not run, turn and jump; he runs, jumps and turns. It is the run in at speed combined with the curve of the run that turns you correctly.

At the end of your run the flat-footed plant of your take-off leg drives you upwards. At this stage make the *inside* leg do all the work, lifting the thigh vigorously upwards and parallel to the bar and continuing *until your chest is facing away from the bar.* (There is no free leg swing in the Flop.)

If you can combine this turning movement with a double-arm swing, you will get tremendous lift. Aim to get the feeling of your head and shoulders going over the bar first, and a forward thrusting of your hips. Don't do what so many novices do: don't jump into the bar in a *sitting* position.

THE CLEARANCE
As you cross the bar, your knees will bend at right angles and your feet will trail. Once you have cleared the upper part of your body and your hips you can, if you watch, see when you need to pull your legs up from the bar. Your speed will bring them clear. With practice you will know just where your body is in relation to the bar and when to pull your legs up.

approach and take-off

free leg swing

double-arm lift

High jump: the basic action

For years high jumpers were taught how to clear the bar but never really how to clear it once it had become *high*. There has now been a complete change in the way athletes tackle this event. Coaches now stress the importance of the *run-up* and *take-off* much more strongly, and the actual technique of clearing the bar rather less (though of course it cannot be ignored altogether).

Over the past seventy years high jumping styles have been dictated by changing fashion and changing rules. Now that the only rule of note controlling the actual manner of jumping is the *one-footed take-off rule,* some of the older styles of clearing the bar have been abandoned, and some new ones have emerged. Scissors, Eastern Cut Off, Western Roll, Straddle and the Flop are names probably well known to would-be high jumpers. Now the Eastern Cut Off has disappeared completely and the Western Roll, though it can still be seen occasionally, is more or less defunct. This leaves three principle styles: scissors, straddle and the Flop.

HOW A HIGH JUMPER GAINS HEIGHT
Four factors help a jumper to gain height:
  1. A measured, disciplined approach run.
  2. A flat-footed plant of the take-off foot.
  3. A good free leg swing.
  4. A double-arm lift.

All four apply (with slight differences in emphasis) to scissors, straddle and Flop alike. But remember that every jump is made up of an even-flowing sequence of certain basic elements: the *approach run,* the *'plant',* the *take-off,* the *clearance* and the *landing.* It is even more important to remember that it is the *approach run,* the *plant* and the *take-off* that really decide how high you jump. If these three phases are poor, then not even the most stylish looking clearance will do much for your performance. So work at the big three.

Straddle

In straddle jumping you clear the bar by draping your body closely round the bar and clearing your trailing leg by rotating away from it. As the rotation continues you eventually land on your shoulder blades or your back. It is not just the clearance of straddle that is efficient; the run-up and preparation for take-off and the actual action at take-off all combine to give an efficient jump.

clearance

rotate and feel for pit

LEARNING THE STRADDLE
Unlike the scissor jumper the straddler takes off from the *inside* leg (the one nearest the bar). This may mean that you will approach the bar from the side opposite that you used for scissors — though this does not necessarily follow.

ANGLE OF APPROACH
The angle of approach in straddle is wider than for a scissor jump, and will be somewhere between 25° and 35°. You can now see why it was useful to learn the basics of high jumping with scissors, where you learned to run the last three strides on flat feet and to count out the strides as you did so. In straddle the pattern is the same and you should get into the habit of saying *'heel, heel, heel'* on the last three strides — not because you complete the run on your heels but because it will remind you to approach *on flat feet*. With a five-stride approach, for example, the count will be: *'toe, toe, heel, heel, heel'*.

The purpose of the run is to be fast at the bar. By increasing the length of your run, you increase the speed at the bar.

HOW TO KEEP YOUR JUMP VERTICAL
It is often difficult to persuade novice high jumpers that the event is a *vertical* jump. Too often they prefer to use a fast, uncontrolled approach, taking off far too far away from the bar and landing well beyond it on the other side.

To get a vertical jump you must come in flat-footed on the last three strides so that your take-off leg is able to drive upwards. Think of your take-off leg as a spring that has to be compressed in order to drive you into the air as it recoils.

On the last three strides there is a feeling of your legs being in front of your body. It is vital that the shoulder nearest the bar doesn't drop and cause you to rotate *before* take-off. Keep your chest squarely to the front until after take-off, and swing your free leg up and over the bar.

In the learning stages it is best to put the bar at a low level and for jumpers approaching from the left to say *'take off on the left — land on the right — and roll'*.

For jumpers approaching from the right the message is *'take off on the right — land on the left — and roll'*.

If you do this you will make sure that your free leg is swung upwards leading the rest of your body.

DOUBLE-ARM LIFT
Top-line straddle jumpers use a double-arm lift coinciding with the swing of the free leg to give them extra height. This is a useful but difficult thing to learn. It is best therefore for a novice to let the arms balance the legs.

'FEELING FOR THE PIT'
While you are over the bar, with your chest facing the ground, the only thing left for you to do is to clear your trailing leg. Once you have reached this phase of the jump it is a fairly simple thing to do. Just 'feel for the pit' with your shoulder blade — the right shoulder if you are a left-footed jumper, and the left if you are a right-footed jumper. The rotation of this movement will bring your trailing leg clear. There is no need to lift your head or jerk your trailing leg outwards. In fact, by doing so you are more likely to displace the bar.

Pole vault: learning the event

As in other jumps the approach and take-off really decide whether the jump is a good one or not.

Holding the pole as shown in the illustration on the next page, make a controlled and carefully measured approach run down the middle of the runway. Keep your chest facing squarely forward and the pole steady. Always have a helper standing by. He can steady the pole for you in the learning stage, and catch it before it falls to the ground when you discard it.

All good vaulters use fibre glass poles, but as these are more expensive than metal poles the tendency is still for young vaulters to begin with metal alloy poles. Some coaches believe, in fact, that metal vaulting techniques must be mastered before the vaulter progresses to fibre glass.

The techniques and illustrations in these pages are of *metal* vaulting.

THE ORIGINS OF THE POLE VAULT
Originally pole vaulting was a practical skill used by our ancestors when, for example, they wanted to cross a stream which had neither shallows nor foot-bridge. Clearly, in such circumstances the pole was needed to 'convey' the vaulter, in fact to give him a ride. 'Riding' still forms the basis of pole vaulting technique, and in the early stages it can be quite difficult to learn.

COMING DOWN TO GO UP
Strangely, your first attempts at pole vaulting can be learned by coming down rather than by going up.

Stand on a grass bank and put the pole down on to the flat ground at the foot of it. Now swing down from the bank holding on to the pole. It will support you and take you for a 'ride'. As soon as you feel it taking you with it you will feel a natural inclination to let go. Resist this desire; you need the pole to take you up to heights way beyond your high jumping capacity.

When you have learned to ride the pole you can graduate to practice vaults from the runway into the long jump pit instead of from the bank.

THE GRIP AND CARRY
A very simple guide to novice pole vaulters is to 'hold as high as you can, run as fast as you can, plant and hang on'. That isn't all there is to it of course, but there's a lot of sound practical advice in the instruction.

It is difficult to carry a long pole holding on to the end of it so poles come in different lengths to suit the age and height of the vaulter. A pole of 3.50 metres is a good length for beginners.

The tapering end is the end you hold, and as there

is a danger of hand slip on the bare metal, black adhesive tape is bound round the pole from your lowest gripping point to the highest. As you improve your aim will be to hold the pole higher up. This will come with strength and mastery of the skill, and you will then have to place the tape higher.

The vaulter is usually a fast runner, and the way you hold and carry the pole must be such that your speed is only fractionally reduced by the fact that you are carrying a pole.

The grip: grip the pole so that the bottom hand (the front hand during the carry) faces palm downwards, with fingers over the top of the pole, as shown in the illustration). Your top (rear) hand should be placed about 60cm to 90cm higher up the pole and should *guide* not grip it. The palm of the top hand faces the direction of the run, with the pole fitting into the V formed by your thumb and forefinger.

The carry: first you must decide whether you want to carry the pole on your left side or your right. If you want to carry on the right then your take-off will be a *left-footed* take-off, and if you want to carry on the left your take-off will be a *right-footed* take-off. The decision is usually based on the choice of carry rather than the choice of take-off foot.

The correct carry position is to have the top hand (palm facing the run) below your hip and level with the rear line of the buttock. During your run up, your top hand presses down so that the pole tilts slightly upwards to bring the tip of the pole roughly level with the top of your head. Both arms are kept bent at the elbows as you make your run up but you must not allow any 'pumping' action on the pole.

Your aim must be to keep your chest facing squarely to the front when you run and carry.

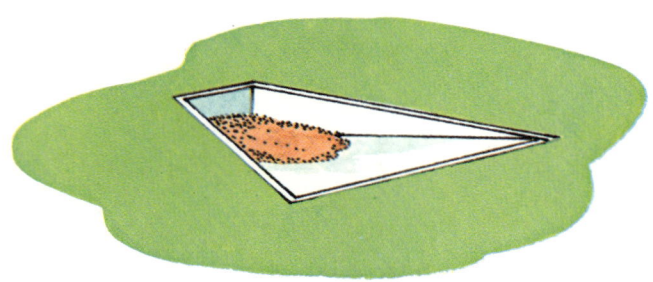

For a valid vault the pole has to be 'planted' in the box set in the ground in front of the bar. For metal vaulting a small quantity of sand is placed in the box to cushion the pole when it strikes the back of the box. A rubber plug on the end of fibre glass poles makes the sand unnecessary.

Hold the pole with your hands about 60 to 90cm apart and so that your thumbs and forefingers form two V's round it.
The palm of your bottom (front) hand faces the ground, the palm of your top (rear) hand faces the direction of your run. During the approach run the *rear* hand guides and steadies the pole, the *front* hand grips it. When you make the plant and the pole hits the back of the box your rear hand *grasps* the pole.

Carry the pole below your hip level with the tip roughly in line with the top of your head. A *left-side* carry gives a *right foot* take-off, and a *right-side* carry gives a *left foot* take-off.

riding the pole

rock and pull

plant and take-off

Pole vault: key phases

turn and push

clear and drop

THE 'PLANT'
Putting the pole into the box is known as 'planting'. As you make the last few strides of your approach run begin to lower the pole ready to make contact with the box. As you make the plant your top hand changes from guiding the pole to grasping it, and the pole is pushed out. It then moves *upwards and forwards.* In metal vaulting your bottom hand then moves up the pole until it almost touches your top hand. (This doesn't happen in fibre glass vaulting because the vaulter's hands remain apart in order to bend the pole.)

THE TAKE-OFF
Make your take-off from *directly underneath your top hand.* This is most important and cannot be stressed too strongly. If your take-off foot is nearer to the box than your body at take-off, you will be snatched off the ground and will start to go up in front of the pole. You will then be up before it and forced to leave it early, and the whole point of using a pole at all will be lost. You must therefore try to stay *behind* the pole, 'ride' it, and then let it take you up with it.

Your take-off foot should be facing straight towards the vault and be in the centre of the runway at the plant. If it gets off centre it means that you have not pushed the pole far enough out before take-off. You will then swing round the side of the pole and, again, be on your way up before the pole is. This must never happen.

THE HANG, PULL-PUSH AND CLEARANCE
'Ride' the pole at take-off, hanging directly behind it as shown in the illustration. If you tuck (bend) your knees at this stage it will produce a bunched position

that will take you straight on into the landing area — but not over the bar! You must therefore learn to wait until your legs start to swing through before quickly tucking your knees up and concentrating on pulling *up the pole* not pulling towards the bar. When your knees reach head height, PULL. The pull takes you forward and you will fly away from the bar.

THE LANDING
How you land will depend on the type of landing area used. On a built-up foam pit you can land how you like, but if the landing area is one of sand, you should take the weight on your legs before rolling over.

THE ESSENTIALS OF POLE VAULT
There are many refinements to pole vaulting but if you learn the basics early you will not find it difficult to make progress.

As in many other athletic activities, work on the ground improves your performance in the air. Put in another way, this means that a good take-off is all important to the actual clearance.

A sound run-up, beginning with five or seven strides, and a low grip are sufficient to enable you to plant and 'ride' the pole from the box. You will soon be ready to reach out to a nine-stride run-up with the pole held higher.

As your speed increases and your grip is placed higher, your take-off position will change because it must still occur with your body vertically below your hands. Check your take-off position repeatedly as you begin to work with a higher handhold.

And finally there is one vital safety measure that all vaulters must observe: *vault only with a pole made by a reputable manufacturer.*

The rules for the throws

There are four throwing events: shot put, discus, javelin and hammer. The first three are open to men, boys, women and girls. Hammer throwing is restricted to men and boys only.

Throwing competitions were in earlier times used as practice games of war, and if safety rules are not carefully observed in competition and training the throws are still capable of maiming and even killing. It is absolutely essential for competitors, officials and spectators to observe the following simple but vital rules:

1. *Never throw an implement when anyone is in or near the landing area.*
2. *Never stand in the landing area when anyone is about to throw.*
3. *Never return any implement to the throwing area by throwing it; always carry it back.*
4. *When working in groups, all throw together and all collect together.*
5. *Always treat javelins with care. They are perhaps the most dangerous implements, even when being carried. Carry them vertically, point downwards. Never run to retrieve them, and when extracting them from the ground, first push them into a vertical position and then lift directly upwards from the ground.*
6. *Keep all throwing implements in good order. Loose discus locking screws and jammed hammer spindles can lead to breakages in use and cause accidents. Prevention is better than cure.*

THE RULES

Order of throwing: the order in which competitors throw is drawn by lots.

Number of throws: in throws competitions each competitor is allowed three throws. First place is awarded to the competitor making the longest throw, second place to the one who makes the second longest throw, and so on. In the event of a tie, the premier place is given to the competitor who has made the longest throw other than the throw which created the tie.

Scratch line: the scratch line is that part of the rim of the throwing circle (in shot, discus and hammer) and that part of the arc (in javelin) adjacent to the landing sector. If the thrower's foot crosses the scratch line a 'no throw' is called.

Landing sector: the landing sector is the area in which the implement must fall for a valid throw. For shot, discus and hammer the sector is a 45° segment of a circle, and for javelin a 29° segment. The diagrams opposite show very clearly the areas into which you must land your throw.

Landing mark: the landing mark must be made by the *head* of the implement. Marks made by the tail of the javelin or the handle of the hammer are not accepted. In discus and javelin it is the duty of the judge to observe as accurately as he can where the implement lands and to measure the throw from that point. Javelins do not have to stick in the ground for the throw to be valid but *they must land point first.*

In the throwing area: in all throws the thrower must *start* and *complete* his throw inside the throwing circle (for discus, hammer and shot) or inside the runway (for javelin). At no time during the throw is the thrower allowed to touch the top rim of the circle or painted part of the scratch line beyond the inside edge or the ground outside them with *any* part of his body. If he does so, a 'no throw' is recorded. In hammer throwing the implement itself is allowed to touch these areas without penalty.

Leaving the throwing area: when the throw has been completed the discus, shot and hammer thrower *must* leave the circle from the *rear* half, and the javelin thrower *must* leave the runway from *behind* the scratch line. In all four events if the thrower leaves the circle or the runway *before* the implement lands, the throw is invalid.

Measuring the throw: the throw is measured from the edge of the landing mark nearest to the scratch line. Hold the zero end of the tape at the edge of the landing mark. Pass the running end over the scratch line and read off the distance thrown at the edge of the scratch line farthest from the mark.

For discus, javelin and hammer, the distances are measured to the nearest 2cm below that shown on the tape; for shot put the measurement is made to the nearest centimetre.

THE IMPLEMENTS

Start with light implements and progress to the heaviest you can handle *comfortably*. Trying to throw implements which are too heavy for you during the early learning stages creates many unnecessary problems, and can seriously harm your later progress.

Details of the correct competition weights for your age are available from the schools' or national governing body.

Opposite: the red areas on the diagrams indicate the throwing sectors for shot put (*A*), discus and hammer (*B*), and javelin (*C*). If the implement lands outside these sectors it is a no throw.

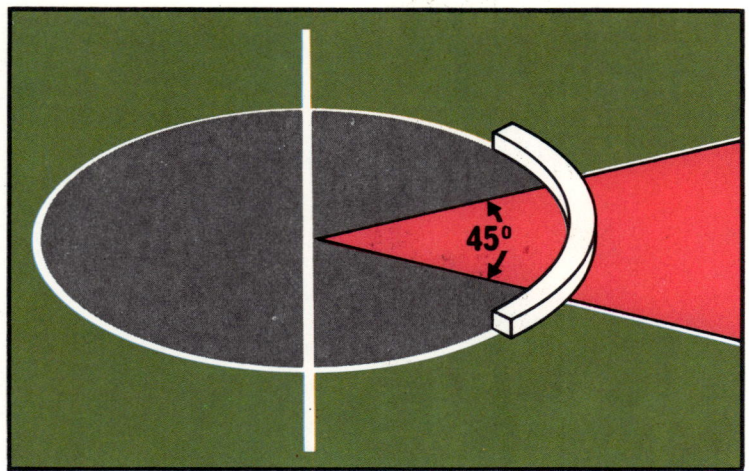

The shot and hammer circles are 2·135m in diameter, while the discus circle is 2·5m. In all three events the athlete must retire from the rear half of the circle after his throw. Failure to do so brings disqualification. The 'stop board' is used in shot put only, and the athlete is allowed to touch only its inside edge.

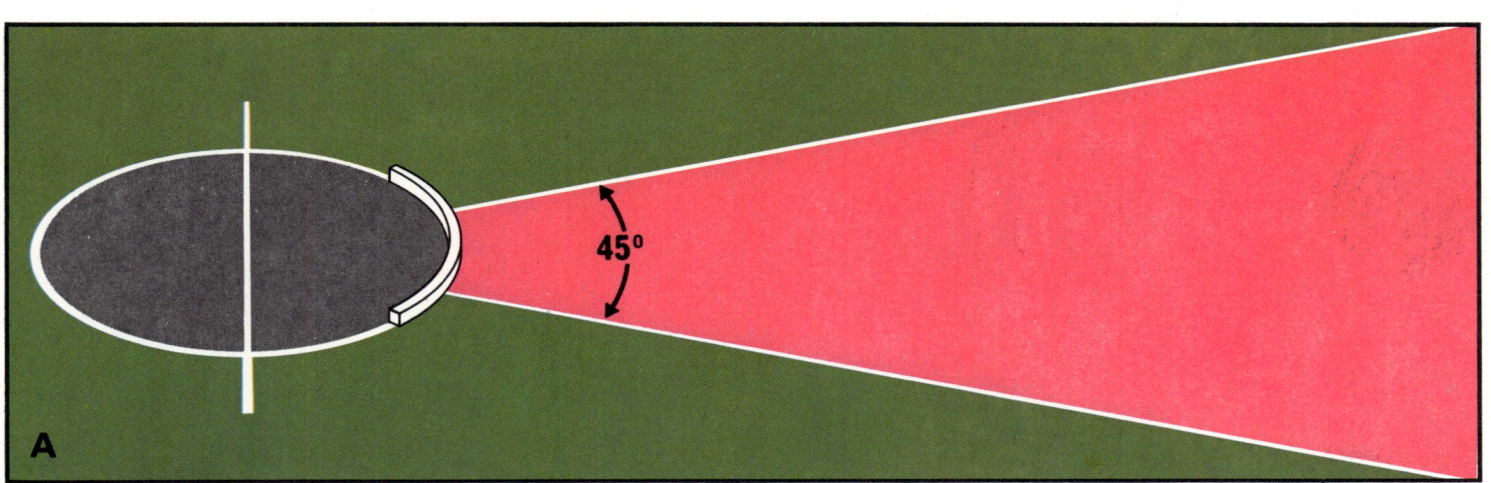

A

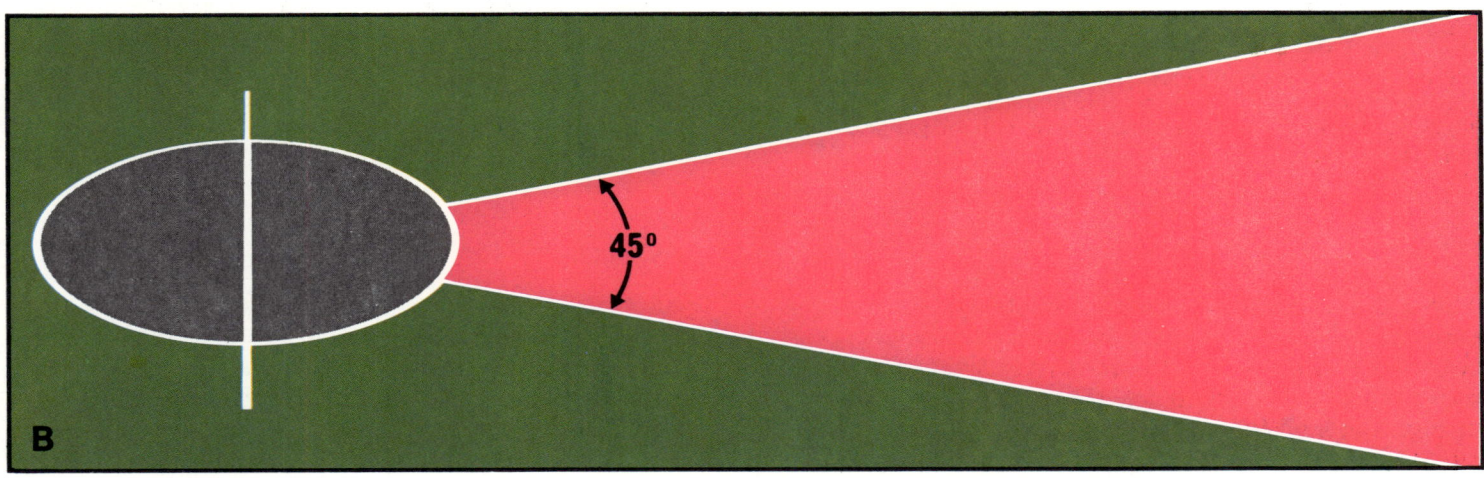

B

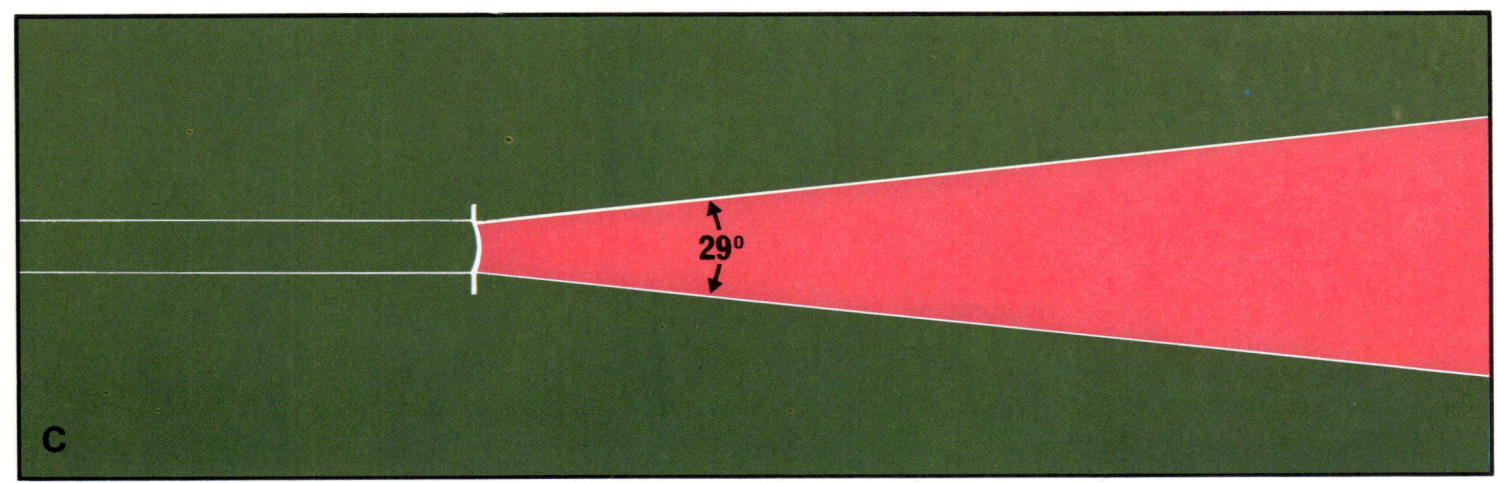

C

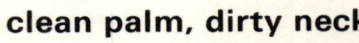
clean palm, dirty neck

basic stance

Shot put: learning the event

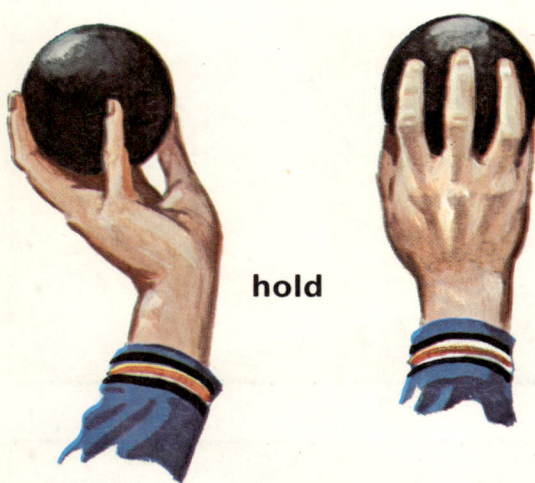

hold

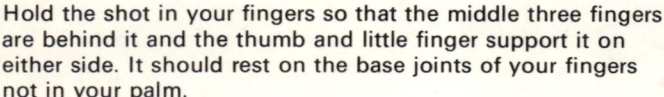

Hold the shot in your fingers so that the middle three fingers are behind it and the thumb and little finger support it on either side. It should rest on the base joints of your fingers not in your palm.

Cradle the shot in to your neck and keep the elbow of your throwing arm high.

Shot put is a 'pushing' event. The rules state that the shot must be held 'in close proximity to the chin and the hand shall not be dropped below this position during the act of putting. The shot must not be brought behind the line of the shoulders'.

In effect, this means that the shot must not be *thrown*.

The putting techniques of modern top-class shot putters are based on complex mechanics and require a strength and a suppleness that the average beginner does not possess. Their finely balanced timing takes years to achieve. You can, however, develop an effective *simpler* technique from which you will be able to progress as you move into higher levels of competition.

THE PUTTING ACTION
There are two main elements in the shot put action: the *shift* and the *lift*.

The *shift* is the movement that takes the thrower from a *starting* position at the *rear* of the throwing circle to his *delivery* position at the *centre*. Its purpose is to give the shot initial motion, so that when the

final effort is made the thrower is *adding to speed it already has* instead of trying to move it from rest.

The *lift* is made at the moment the thrower's front foot touches the ground behind the stop board, and is made primarily by the rear leg, accompanied by a vigorous twist of the hips in the direction of the throw. The rear leg and hip actions add speed to the shot and are followed by a bracing of the front side of the thrower's body, which increases the shot speed still further until the throwing arm extends explosively in the direction of the throw. The thrower keeps contact with the shot through his wrist and hand until the last moment. In this way he 'works' against the shot for as long as he possibly can before delivery in order to throw further.

THE HOLD
Hold the shot in your fingers so that the middle three fingers are behind it, and your thumb and little finger support it on each side.

Place the shot against your neck, in the hollow formed where your collar bone meets your neck, so that your fingers are behind the shot and you are able

prop

rotate

strike

chase

First try a standing put. Without using your legs, put the shot as far as you can. Try to increase the twist of the upper part of your body to improve the distance you throw.

to push it forwards. A good shot putter always has a clean palm and a dirty neck! The elbow of your throwing arm should be held high, almost in line with your shoulder.

STANDING PUT

Stand facing the direction of the throw and push the shot out as far as you can using only your arm. Take a number of throws and mark your best effort. Next, take up the same position and do the same again but this time *bend your legs* and use them *before* your arm. You will almost certainly find that your shot goes further, proving that use of the legs is vital to long throwing. Never forget it!

Now increase the range over which you are able to keep contact with the shot by taking up a position facing forwards with flexed legs, but this time turn slowly through 90° to the rear, keeping your hips as near as possible in their original position. Chase the shot out with your arm and keep your elbow high. Try to work LEGS – TRUNK – ARM. Once again the distance of your put should improve.

Next take up the stance as in the top illustration

on page 46. Your rear foot should be on the centre line pointing back to 10 o'clock, if you visualise the circle as a clock face looking at it from your position at the centre. The rear of the circle, then, is at 12 o'clock. Your front (left) foot should be offset slightly to the right so that your hips can drive forward during the throw. In this position the toe of your left foot should be in line with the heel of your right foot, and your rear leg should be flexed (bent) at the knee so that your head, knee and rear foot are in vertical alignment. Beware of bending your back to achieve this starting position, and look *back*, not down.

When you throw, use explosive legs! Think LEGS – TRUNK – ARM. Avoid letting your left side collapse when the shot leaves your hand. If this fault occurs you can correct it by concentrating on hanging your free (left) arm from a 'sky-hook' until after the shot has gone, or on keeping your shoulders horizontal.

This, then, is the standing put. You should be able to throw quite a long way with it before learning the 'shift'. Remember that the purpose of the shift is to give the shot initial impetus, and at best it can only improve a good basic put.

Shot put

the basic stance

chin, knee and toe in line

left toe offset
(in line with right heel)

delivery: feet down,
shoulder high

THE SHIFT

Without using the shot, take up the position for a standing throw but nearer the rear of the circle than before. Place your rear foot halfway between the centre of the circle and the rim at the rear. Your front foot will move correspondingly nearer the rear edge of the circle. Take most of your weight on your rear leg and overbalance slowly in the direction of the front of the circle by letting your rear leg collapse slightly. At the same time push your seat back as if you were about to sit in a chair placed behind you. When you feel the pressure in your rear foot move from the toes to the heel, *push hard in the direction of the stop board.* Pull your rear foot quickly under yourself and land, *right-left,* in the front half of the circle. You should now be at the front of the circle in the position for a standing put.

Repeat this practice until you feel balanced and comfortable doing it. When you do, take up the shot and execute a complete put – shift *and* lift.

shift and lift

legs — trunk — arm

The throwing action takes place through your rear leg, which lifts your body as your hips drive forward.

**the chase:
get on to front foot**

WHAT TO AIM FOR IN THE SHIFT

Work for fast feet followed by a good rear leg lift at the centre of the circle. As your strength and ability improve, gradually move your starting position towards the rear of the circle. Improvement in your puts will depend on your ability to achieve a good putting position at the centre. Do not, however, fall into the trap of letting this position become a *static* one. Once the shot has started on its 'journey' from the rear of the circle it should not stop until it hits the ground far away from your feet.

Keep low, looking to the rear, during the shift — certainly until both feet are in contact with the ground at the end of the shift phase. As your rear leg lifts at the centre, drive your hip forward in the direction of the throw. *Your hip should always lead your shoulders and arm.*

When you reach the front of the circle, keep your feet on the ground, get your body weight over your front foot, and chase the shot out with your hand until the last possible moment.

basic throwing position

Javelin:
learning the event

heels well down

Keep your throwing arm up and the javelin close to your ear.
Land on flexed legs, heels down and hip forward.

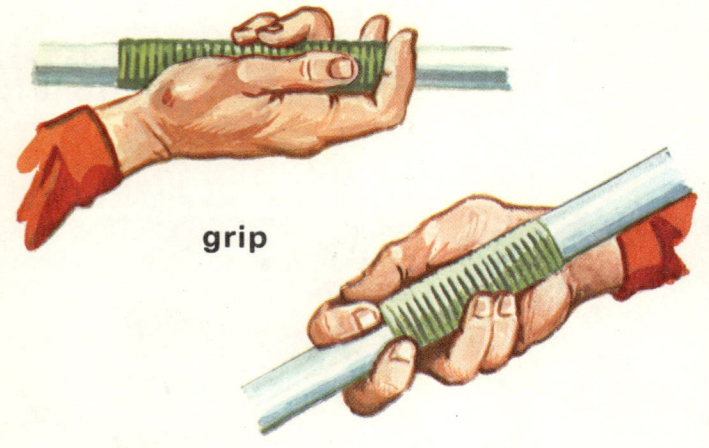

grip

Just as shot putting is a *pushing* event, so javelin throwing is a *pulling* event. The rules state that 'the javelin must be held at the grip with one hand only so that the little finger is nearest the point. The javelin shall be thrown over the shoulder, and must not be slung or hurled'.

The javelin is the only throwing event which does not take place from inside a throwing circle, and the only one in which the thrower is allowed what is virtually an unlimited approach run before releasing the implement. It is the run up that gets the javelin under way before the thrower gives the final impulse.

It is important to mention that while the thrower may run *on* or *outside* the run-up lines, the rules require him to be *behind the arc and between the run-up lines at the actual moment of throwing*.

THE THROWING ACTION
The basic action is simple to describe, though less easy to perform well: the thrower makes his approach

run down the runway and delivers (or releases) the javelin explosively as he reaches the scratch line.

The run-up has a running or *'carry'* phase and a *pre-delivery* (or pre-throw) phase.

The carry phase: during the running or carry phase the javelin is carried parallel to the ground, high above the thrower's shoulder, elbow tucked underneath the javelin and palm turned skywards.

The pre-delivery phase: this begins five strides before the actual delivery or release of the javelin and, if the thrower is right handed, starts as his left foot comes forward. As it does so, the thrower begins to withdraw his carrying arm behind his shoulder and at the same time turns his shoulders at right angles to the direction of his throw, and begins to run *on his heels.* A long last stride in the pre-delivery phase gives him a distinct backwards lean, at which point, about 6 to 8 metres from the scratch line, the delivery phase proper begins.

The delivery phase: from the broad base given him by the long last stride of the pre-delivery phase the thrower's right leg and hip drive powerfully forward, his upper body unwinds and his arm brings the javelin forward with a flail-like action.

This description is, again, a very rough picture of the carefully timed and balanced action needed for a good throw. The illustrations on the next page show much more clearly the real nature of the event.

As with other throws, the best way to learn the whole technique is to learn first how to perform a good standing throw, and to progress from that to a simple run-and-throw with correct withdrawal of your carrying arm. Finally, from these basic elements you will be able to forge a useful and sound technique.

THE GRIP

The correct javelin grip is best described as a 'claw grip' or — more topically — as a 'Harvey Smith' grip.

Hold the javelin just behind the binding so that the shaft lies along the palm of your hand, with your little finger nearest the point, and place your first and second fingers on either side of the shaft. Slide your hand forward until these two fingers rest against the edge of the binding. Grip it naturally with your thumb and remaining fingers. Make sure that your grip is spread along the binding so that only the end joints of your first and second fingers rest against the edge of the binding.

THE STANDING THROW

Stand, feet apart, right foot behind left, *so that both point in the direction of the throw.* Hold the javelin high above your throwing shoulder, palm upwards and elbow under the javelin. The javelin should be in line with an imaginary target on the ground about five metres beyond your front foot.

Withdraw your throwing arm, keeping your palm turned skywards still, and hollow your back slightly to 'string the bow'. Keep your throwing hand high and your arm slightly flexed. Pull on the javelin to project it vigorously towards the imaginary target.

Next, try to use your legs and upper body before your arm, and work to apply power *directly along the shaft.* Check the landing attitude of the javelin. If you applied force correctly through the implement, the tail will be staring you straight between the eyes. If, on the other hand, it is inclined to right or left or vertically then the force has been wasted uselessly *across* the line of flight instead of *along* it.

standing throw

2

1

3

1. Stand feet apart. 2. Arch your back and withdraw your carrying arm. 3. Step forward and drive the javelin hard at an imaginary target on the ground five metres ahead of you.

Now you can move on to the *running throw*. The starting position is the same as for the standing throw, except that your forward leg is on your *throwing arm* side (the right leg for a right-handed thrower, and the left leg for a left-handed thrower).

Now withdraw your throwing arm *before* moving your feet at all, and jog three strides: *left — right — left.* Keep your feet and hips pointing forwards in the direction of your throw, and hold the javelin well back. As your left foot lands on the final stride — THROW.

Work to keep the javelin well back, and pull from as far behind you as you possibly can. *Land on your heels,* and *keep both feet down* until the javelin has left your hand.

At this stage, once you are reasonably proficient, you are ready to aim for another imaginary target to teach yourself the correct angle of release. Imagine you are trying to land the javelin on top of a tree or the roof of a building at an angle of 35° from your throwing point, and aim to put it into a flight path along that line. If you can do this, then the javelin is so designed that, as it loses speed, it will change its flight attitude, begin to descend and land point first. It requires no further help from you! If you consciously aim to land it point first it will only reduce the distance of your throw.

ready

b...

PRE-DELIVERY PHASE

Next, to this basic throw add two more strides to produce a five-stride run up: *left — right — left — right — throw*, with the throw and the last left stride taking place *simultaneously*. Again, withdraw your arm *before* you begin your run. Drive your throwing hip hard into the direction of your throw at the beginning of the throwing action (as in discus throwing) but brace your *non-throwing* leg and keep that shoulder high throughout the release.

When you have mastered this, change your action at the start of the run, so that you now withdraw the javelin *as you take the first step,* and not before. Count to yourself as you move . . . *BACK — two — three — four — throw.*

By now you should be throwing successfully from a run and will have a technique that is acceptable at competition level. This can be developed still further by adding four (and possibly a further four) 'carry' strides to give you a nine- (or thirteen) stride approach. Your starting position will in each instance be the same as that already used for the five-stride approach. Beginning the run with your non-throwing foot, jog four strides with the javelin in the carry position: *one — two — three — four*. Then, as your left foot comes forward on the *fifth* stride, withdraw the javelin to begin the pre-delivery phase, and complete the throw . . . *BACK — two — three — four — throw*

Javelin: th...

four

THROW...

TRAINING TIPS

Work to keep the javelin in correct alignment during all stages of the throw. Don't allow your grip to slacken or your hand or arm to drop during the pre-throw phase. Try hard to produce 'fast feet' on the last stride, landing *heel down,* with legs flexed. Remember, too, to leave the javelin well back when you have withdrawn your throwing arm until your legs, hips and upper body have 'worked' on it.

two

three

unning throw

Start with right leg forward. Start running with left leg. Withdraw *five* strides before delivery as the left leg goes forward. Land on your heels — with legs flexed — and keep your hips to the front.

There are no rules special to discus throwing that need concern you once you have studied the rules applying to throwing events in general given on page 42.

Discus throwing is basically a 'slinging' action made after a running turn across the circle. The turn in discus, like the shift in shot put, serves to give movement to the implement before you apply the final effort.

Because the discus is aerodynamic in shape it will fly much better and much further when it is presented at the right angle and in the right direction in relation to the prevailing wind. When the throw is executed correctly the air passes above and below the discus (as shown in the diagram), creating lift, just as it does with, say, the wing of an aircraft. But when the discus is presented at a wrong flight angle, the air acts as a brake and reduces both speed and distance. The correct flight angle to aim for is at 40° to the horizontal.

Discus: learning the event

basic throw

hold

feet well apart for broad throwing base

THE THROWING ACTION

The athlete takes up an upright position at the rear of the circle, *facing away from the direction of the throw,* with feet shoulder-width apart and the discus resting loosely in the fingers of the throwing hand. After one or two loose preliminary swings, he makes a pivoting turn on the balls of both feet to bring him to the front of the circle where his body unwinds fast. This releases the 'wound up' arm to send the discus into a soaring trajectory before the athlete checks his own forward motion to prevent fouling the scratch line and thereby making a 'no throw'.

THE HOLD

Hold the discus so that it rests loosely in your throwing hand with fingers spread and only the end joints wrapped over the rim. Your thumb should rest lightly across the back of the discus. The important thing to remember is that the discus should be held, *not gripped*.

As the discus is released it should leave your hand by rolling across your first finger. You can get the feeling of this by holding the discus vertically in front of you, supported if necessary by your non-throwing hand. Push upwards with the little finger of your throwing hand and the discus will roll across your first finger and out of your hand on to the ground.

THE THROW

The very best way to learn discus is to build up from a simple standing throw to a correctly executed running turn.

Standing throw 1: stand facing the direction of the throw with feet apart and one foot behind the other. Hold the discus down by your thigh at arm's length. Transfer your weight forwards and backwards, moving your throwing arm with you. As you rock forwards release the discus *vertically* off your first finger so that it spins into the air.

Repeat this a time or two and try to throw as high as you can, still keeping the feeling of the discus rolling across your finger.

Standing throw 2: now turn 90° to the rear so that you present your *non-throwing* side to the direction of

In the early learning stages practise spinning the discus off your first finger vertically.

Centrifugal force will cause the discus to remain in your hand as you swing, just as it keeps water in a bucket swung round your head.

flight

1

2

3

Discus: turn and throw

standing throw

1

2

3

4

Take up a stationary position (1). Step back into the offset feet position with your throwing arm 'wound up' (2). Use your hips and legs to initiate a slinging horizontal release (3 & 4).

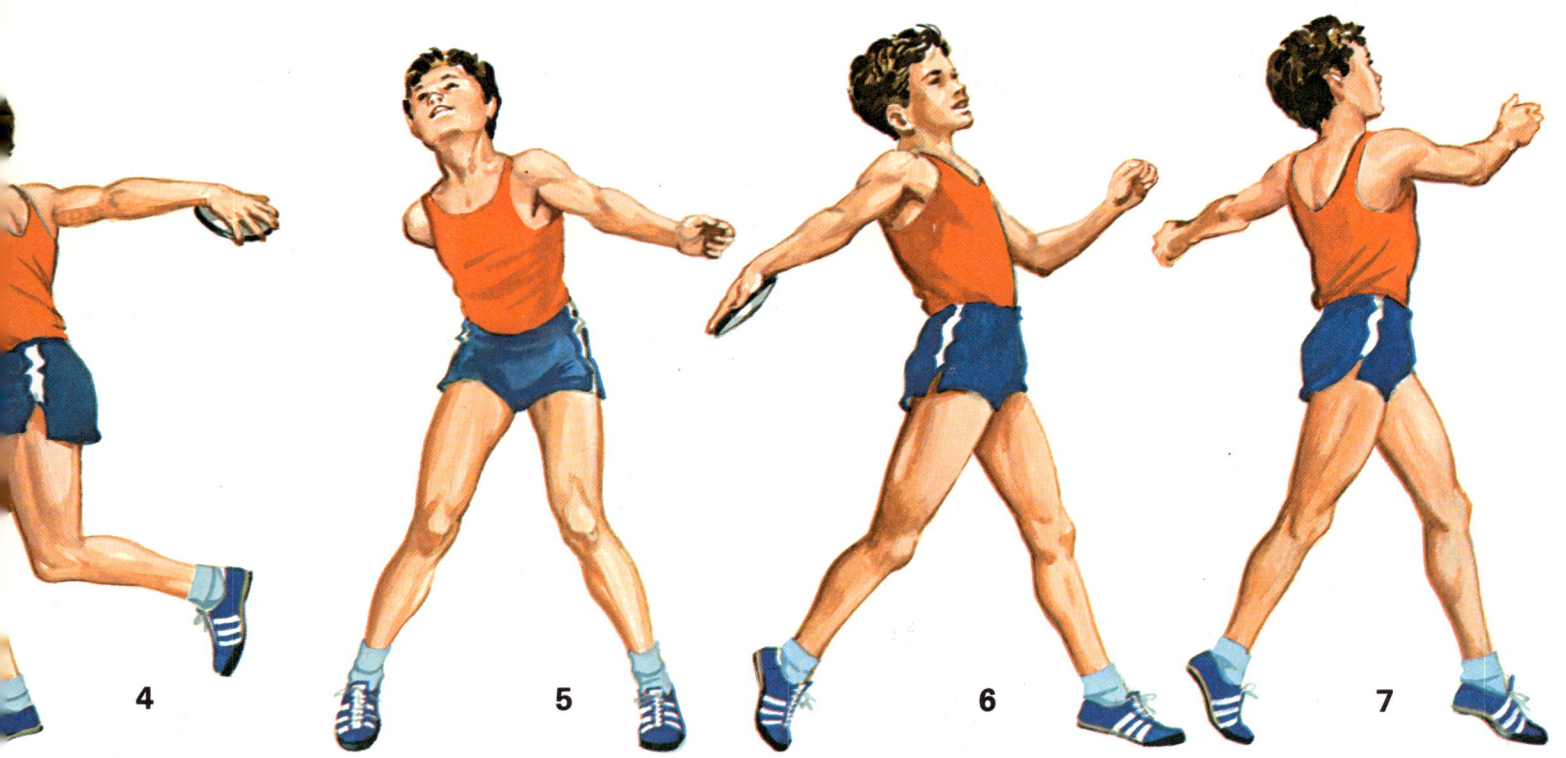

4   5   6   7

'Run' round your left foot, away from your throwing arm (1 & 2). Pick up your right foot (3) and place it near the centre of the circle (4) while your left foot follows and is placed behind the rim. Initiate the throw with your legs and hips (5 & 6). Finish high over your front foot (7).

the throw. Your feet should be shoulder-width apart and pointing in the new direction in which you are facing. Hold the discus with your throwing hand on top and supported underneath by the other. Swing a straight throwing arm horizontally behind your shoulder and at the same time take away the support of your non-throwing hand as you transfer your weight on to your rear foot. Return your weight to your front foot and sling the discus *horizontally*.

Don't be afraid that the discus may fall once you remove the supporting hand. The bucket-of-water principle illustrated on the previous page applies to the discus. The same force that keeps the water in the bucket will keep the discus in your hand *as long as it is kept moving*.

Important points to remember are:
1. Keep an offset foot position with the toe of your front foot in line with the heel of your rear foot.
2. The weight of your body must be over a *flexed* rear leg.
3. The discus must be withdrawn before throwing.
4. Your throwing arm must be kept extended (stretched) during the 'slinging' action.

Standing throw 3: now try to increase the range over which you 'work' on the discus. You will have to pivot on both feet to do this. As you transfer your weight on to your front foot during the throw, exaggerate the pivot to the front by thrusting your rear hip forcefully in the direction of the throw. If there is a secret to discus throwing, it is in becoming 'hip conscious'.

THE TURN
Once you have mastered the standing throw and the

balance problems it poses, you can try turning.

Turning without the discus: try first to turn *without* the discus, adopting the position used for *standing throw*, that is, with feet facing the direction of the throw.

Rock forwards and backwards and as you move forwards take a little jump to land *right/left*, with your left foot landing slightly ahead of your right.

When you have had some practice at this, repeat the action but this time add a tight turn in the air so that you land with your feet and shoulders *facing the rear*. This should be a *gentle* movement in which the lower part of your body and your feet should move before your upper body. To increase your awareness of this movement, point your right arm forward in the direction of the throw at shoulder level and turn 'under' it, *keeping it fixed and pointing in the direction of the throw*.

Keep the movement relaxed and work for fast, tight feet, and good balance.

Turning with the discus: take up the discus and after one or two preliminary rocks forwards and backwards, *turn and throw*. When you are familiar with this, take up a position inside the circle at the rear, with your front (left) foot pointing in the direction of the throw and your rear (right) foot at right angles to it. Keep the toe of your rear foot close to the heel of your front foot. Now jump-turn, running around your front foot, and *throw*.

Work at this turning movement, aiming to achieve good balance throughout the throw, with fast, tight feet and a good braced left side at the moment of delivery. *Never* let your left shoulder drop at any stage of the throw.

Hammer: learning the event

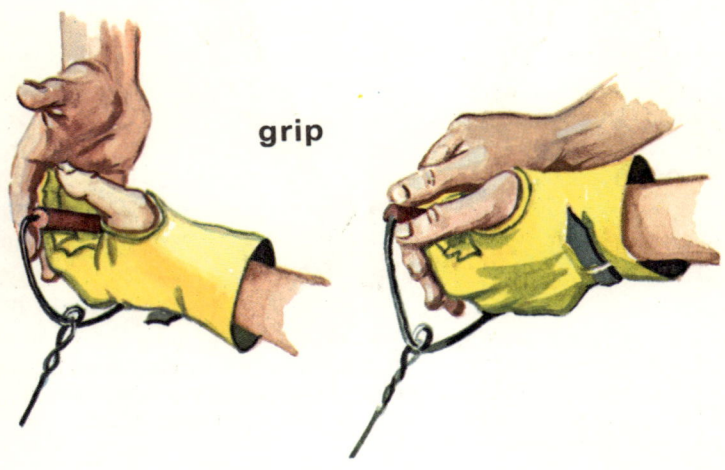

grip

delivery

The hammer throw is the least well known of the throwing events but it is worth the close attention of the smaller athlete interested in throwing. At top-class level the shot put, discus and, to some extent, the javelin have become events very much dominated by the *big* men. But because of the gymnastic skill it requires the hammer can still offer an opening (even at Olympic level) for the good *little* man (there is no hammer event for women or girls).

The hammer itself is descended from the agricultural sledgehammer. But to describe what is now a sophisticated piece of modern engineering simply as 'a shot attached to a handle by a wire' is to do it less than justice.

The overall length of the hammer must not be more than 121.5cm and the head must be spherical. It is thrown from a circle of the same dimensions as for shot put (but without a stop board) and into a 45° landing sector (the same as for discus). For safety reasons it is desirable that all hammer throws are made from a cage or enclosure.

THE HAMMER GLOVE
The hammer thrower is the only athlete permitted by the rules to wear protective clothing: a leather glove on the hand in direct contact with the hammer handle. Although special gloves can be bought, smooth on back and front, and open at the finger tips to conform to the rules, an old kid glove will suffice during the early years of throwing.

At release keep your feet down and your arms long, and lift hard with your legs. Finish on tiptoe with your hands overhead.

THE THROWING ACTION

The thrower takes up a starting position at the rear of the circle *with his back to the direction of the throw*, and in the course of a series of complex swings and turns builds up force in the hammer until the moment of release, by which time *he is facing the direction of the throw*.

The whole emphasis of the throw lies in working the lower part of the body under the upper half, tightly and in perfect balance, while trying to keep the arms long and the head of the hammer as far away from the thrower's turning axis as possible. Slow, deliberate swings build up gradually into ever-accelerating turns, culminating in a final explosive lift.

LEARNING THE EVENT

Hammer is a complex event to teach and to learn. The skill of turning takes time to perfect and until it is mastered you will not experience the true thrill of the event.

Many attempts have been made to give learners something of the real feel of throwing before they have mastered the turns. So far they have all been hindered by the same difficulty, that of using the full-length implement. The method now suggested overcomes this problem, and has already been particularly successful in teaching young throwers. It requires the removal of the hammer wires and their replacement by a ¾ in (2cm) mild steel 'D' shackle. The head is then fixed directly to the handle by means of the shackle. With this shortened version it is possible to get much closer to the real feeling of hammer throwing before you learn to turn.

THE GRIP

Hold the handle in your left hand (if you are right handed) so that it rests across the base joints of your fingers, keeping your thumb outstretched and clear. Now place your right hand so that the fingers cover the fingers of your left hand. Finally close your thumbs lightly alongside each other to complete the grip.

THE STANDING THROW

Stand with your feet shoulder-width apart, *facing away from the direction of the throw*, with the hammer held as just described and hanging at arm's length opposite your left thigh. Lift the hammer forwards to chest height on straight arms, and allow it to drop pendulum fashion to the right-hand side. As it starts to swing back from the limit of its pendulum path, lift forcefully with your legs and straight arms, twisting the upper part of your body to the left and pivoting slightly on both toes to release the hammer high over your left shoulder. The hammer should land directly behind you. Transfer your weight to your right foot and to your left with the hammer as you throw.

Stand upright with the hammer head alongside your right foot. Pass the hammer around to the left, keeping your feet firmly fixed and continue passing it around your head. Get the swings going using your arms, then let your hips take over.

incorrect   **correct**

Resist a tendency to pull your shoulders away from the hammer as this shortens the effective radius and reduces the distance of your throw.

learning to counter

swings and turns

2 swings

turn 2

LEARNING TO TURN

Stage 1: still using the 'D' shackle arrangement, repeat the standing throw action, this time with your left foot turned 90° to the left and your weight on your left toe. After the pendulum swing, turn discus-fashion around your left foot, executing a little jump-turn . . . *right/left* . . . before releasing the hammer high over your left shoulder.

Work for balanced, easy turning and a good final lift.

Stage 2: this involves turning *heel-toe* on your left foot instead of on the toe alone. This time turn through 180° on your left heel before transferring your weight on to the toe immediately before the jump-turn.

The closer you keep your right leg to your left leg during the turn the quicker the right will regain contact with the ground, and the more time you will have to concentrate on getting a really strong delivery.

Stage 3: Finally, omit the jump-turn altogether by turning a further 180° after the initial 180° rotation on your left heel once the weight has been taken on the toe of your left foot. In this way your left foot never leaves the ground. The right pivots on the toe during the first 180° of rotation, and is lifted from the ground during the second 180°.

When you can manage this 360° turn effectively, you have learned the rudiments of turning. Practise the turns *without the hammer* for ten to fifteen minutes at the beginning of each training session until you can join 3-4-5-6 turns together in one unbroken flowing movement. Work hard to achieve good balance during these practices and avoid, particularly, any temptation to watch your feet.

WORKING WITH A LONGER HAMMER

The hammer can now be progressively lengthened by exchanging the 'D' shackle for a length of nylon cord looped though both the handle and the spindle to give an overall length of first 75cm, then 1 metre, and finally the maximum 121.5cm. At the last stage the nylon cord should be replaced by the proper wire. Nylon cord is, however, quite safe at the shorter lengths providing that it has a breaking strength of over 160kg and is replaced immediately any sign of chaffing is noticed.

LEARNING THE SWING

When you are working with the 1-metre hammer it becomes possible to introduce 'swings' into the skill. Although it is easiest to swing the hammer using your arms only, this is not a good technique to develop since a good hammer thrower works primarily with his *legs*, even during the swings. Your arms should be used merely as rope-like extensions of the wire to 'attach' the hammer to your shoulders.

COUNTERBALANCING THE HAMMER

Counterbalancing the hammer with the lower part of your body can be learned easily. This is an important skill and can be learned in the following way:

Stand upright with the hammer head alongside your right foot and approximately six inches away from it, with the wire held vertically. This means that your hands grasp the hammer just opposite your right hip. Pass the hammer round to the left, that is, anti-clockwise, keeping your feet firmly fixed. As the hammer passes behind your head and back, try to keep it as close to the ground as you possibly can. This can be most easily achieved by turning your shoulders in the opposite direction to the hammer, while keeping your hands moving with it.

When you are able to complete a number of successive swings like this, check to feel what is happening to your hips when the hammer is at its 'high point' (i.e. behind your back) and again when it is at its 'low point' (i.e. off your right foot). In each of these positions you should be able to feel that your hips move *away* from the hammer.

Set the swings going using your arms and then let your hips take over by concentrating on keeping the

entry to turns

turn 1

turn 3

delivery

hip-counter going and forgetting your arms. This is the secret of swinging correctly.

LINKING THE TURNS TO THE SWINGS
The final stage of learning to throw the hammer is to link turns and swings.

Stand at the rear of the circle, as for a standing throw, with the hammer head by your right foot. Swing *twice* in a relaxed manner, keeping the low point opposite your right foot. From the low point at the end of the second swing, keep your hands low and allow your arms to stretch out in the direction of the hammer as it sweeps across in front of you. When the hammer passes an imaginary mid-line between your feet, act just as if your left foot had become attached to it and begin the heel-toe action of the turns. As you complete each turn your right foot should land on the ground *slightly ahead of the hammer.* Shift your weight on to your left foot as you wait for the hammer to reach the position where you can begin the next turn.

Start with two swings overhead, keeping your feet shoulder width apart. Follow with three turns on your left foot. The first half of the turn is made on your heel, and the second half on your toe. When your right foot lands at the end of the last turn, lift the hammer as hard as you can and release it, keeping your hands high.

Complete two such turns and *throw.*

With enough practice you should be able to complete two swings followed by three turns before releasing the hammer (as shown in the illustration).

During the *swings* you will find a natural tendency for the hammer's low point to move from its correct position off your right foot to an *incorrect* one in front of your body. This can be prevented by turning your shoulders round to the rear as the hammer moves through the high point.

During the *turns* work to land in balance, with your right foot ahead of the hammer, and keep your arms passive until the final lift.

Pentathlon and decathlon

Athletics is really twelve different sports lumped into one under the same general label, with the sprints and field events testing power and skill, and the long and middle distances testing physical endurance and mental stamina. It was therefore natural for athletes to seek a test that measured *all-round* ability. This is what the pentathlon and decathlon do. As a result they are considered the Blue Riband events of the athletics programme.

THE PENTATHLON

The pentathlon is a five-event competition for women and girls in which the events (in competing order) are *hurdles, shot put, high jump, long jump* and *200 metres.* The first three events are usually held on one day, and the last two on the following day, making the event a two-day competition. The programme *can* be completed in a single day if the organisers wish, but this is very strenuous for the athletes and is not often done.

THE DECATHLON

The decathlon is the equivalent all-round test for men and boys, although pentathlon events are sometimes organised for *young* boys to give them experience before graduating to the more demanding decathlon. The ten events in the order in which they are held are: *100 metres, long jump, shot put, high jump* and *400 metres* on the first day; and *hurdles, discus, pole vault, javelin* and *1500 metres* on the second day. As in pentathlon the judges and organisers have the power to alter the order of the events and even to hold them all on the same day. But, again, it is very rare for them to exercise this power.

THE SCORING SYSTEM

A complex system of scoring points in pentathlon and decathlon has been devised by the International Amateur Athletics Federation, the world governing body, and the winner is the athlete who scores the highest *total* number of points. The better the performance, the higher the number of points you score. It is therefore possible to be the *overall* winner without winning any single event.

Competitors are not allowed to opt out of events they are not good at and they are eliminated from further competition if they do so, except where they record three no-jumps in a jumping event or three no-throws in a throwing event.

PREPARATION FOR PENTATHLON/DECATHLON

The A.A.A. Five-Star Award Scheme, which has

hurdles

shot

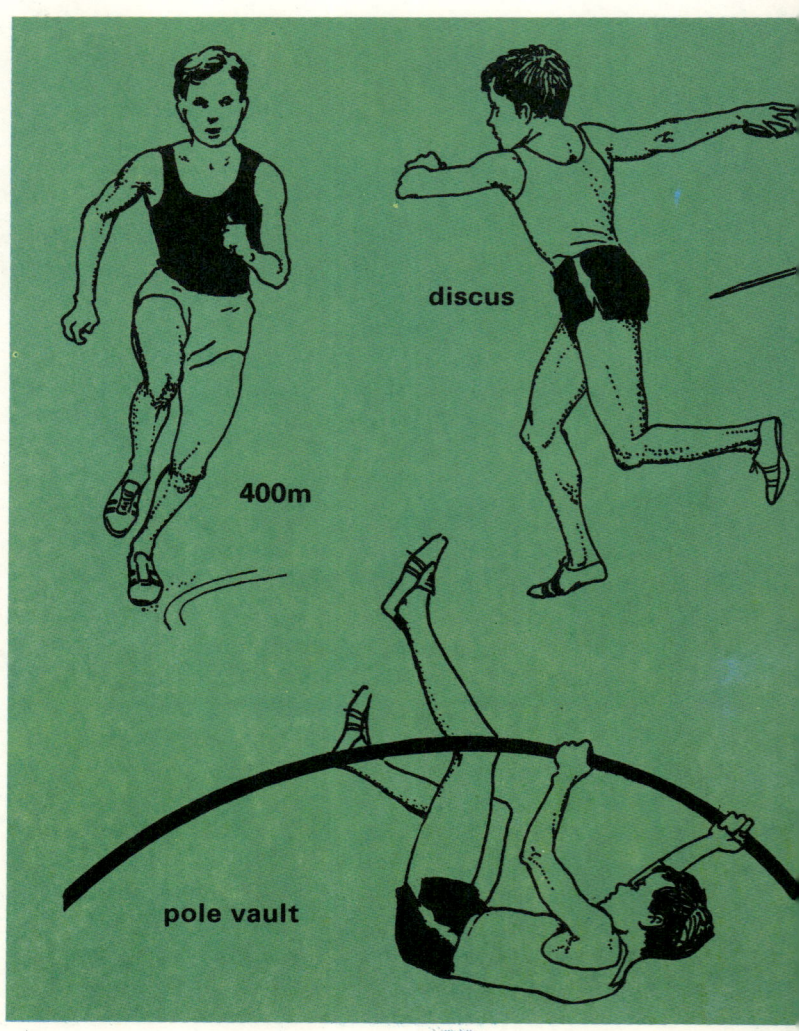

400m

discus

pole vault

high jump

long jump

sprint
(200m in pentathlon
100m in decathlon)

javelin

1500m

proved so popular in schoolboy and schoolgirl athletics in Britain, and which requires performances to be recorded in three events in order to gain an award, has been adapted in recent years to cater for young pentathletes and decathletes, and in fact includes special awards in decathlon and pentathlon. At this level, however, the young athlete participates in ten or five events *of his or her own choice*, of which one must be a jump, one a throw, and one a run.

HOW TO START

The first step for a pentathlete or decathlete who wishes to compete efficiently is to buy a copy of the IAAF scoring tables.

The great problem when you embark on these 'multi-events' is not so much deciding which events to concentrate on but which you can afford to ignore temporarily. There is rarely time to give an equal amount of training time to *all* of them. But two things you *must* be able to do: you must be able to hurdle, and (in decathlon) you must be able to pole vault. If you baulk at the fifth hurdle or are unable to get off the ground in the vault then you have to accept that you have no future at all as an all-rounder.

PROFITABLE IMPROVEMENTS

The quickest and most profitable improvements you can make are in the track events. By improving your track fitness, for example, you can improve in *two-fifths* of the pentathlon (the sprint and the hurdles) and *four-tenths* of the decathlon programme (the 100 metres, 400 metres, the hurdles, and the 1500 metres). You will feel the benefits especially in the 400 metres and the 1500 metres. For example, by improving your 400 metres time by only 5 seconds and your 1500 metres time by 20 seconds, you can gain almost 200 points in each event. Since improvement in one usually brings improvement in the other, an increase of 400 points is easily added to your score.

Similarly, by improving your strength and power levels generally, you will increase your scores in long jump, high jump, shot put, discus and javelin without needing to improve your *technique* in any of them. It is very important to establish right from the beginning a sound basic technique that is good enough to gain a reasonable number of points in each skill event. In practical terms this means that you must have a reliable long jump approach, and a sound high jump clearance without embellishments (most probably the Flop if you have the necessary training facilities with adequate landing areas). Try to add to these a throwing skill that enables you to place your throws consistently down the middle of the landing sector without wasting points by fouling the scratch line.

You can already see that what the pentathlete and the decathlete need are steadiness and persistence rather than flamboyance and flair.

Top: the five pentathlon events.
Bottom: the additional five events for decathlon.